If Those Who Reach Could Touch

If Those
Who Reach
Could Touch

Gail and Gordon
MacDonald

INSIGHT FOR LIVING

MOODY PRESS
CHICAGO

To Ethel and George Akerlow, Gail's mom and dad,
who this year celebrate fifty years of reaching and *touching*.
How grateful we are for their endless support
and modeling of forgiveness and enabling.

Unless noted otherwise, all Scripture quotations are
from the *Holy Bible: New International Version,*
© 1973, 1978 by the International Bible Society. Used
by permission of Zondervan Bible Publishers.

The use of selected references from various versions
of the Bible in this book does not necessarily imply
publisher endorsement of those versions in their en-
tirety.

Library of Congress Cataloging in Publication Data

MacDonald, Gail.
If those who reach could touch.

1. Interpersonal relations. 2. Love. 3. Friendship.
4. Christian life. I. MacDonald, Gordon. II. Title.
HM132.M275   1984   302.3'4   84-4509
ISBN: 0-8024-0426-X

2 3 4 5 6 7 Printing GB Year 88 87 86 85 84

Printed in the United States of America

Contents

Introduction

The family sits quietly in front of the television watching a dramatic presentation that is about to reach its climax. Suddenly the screen goes blank, and we are shocked. What has happened? Soon a message appears: "We have temporarily lost our signal. Please stand by!" We groan and mutter something about timing.

"We have temporarily lost our signal. . . ." One gets the feeling that this sort of thing happens with frightening regularity in many marriages, families, and other relationships. All of us know the pain of that moment when intimacy is lost, rapport dissolves, and the desire to serve is squelched. And many of us have learned what to do at such a time. But just as many of us may not fully understand what has happened or why.

A long time ago the two of us made a decision. We would make relationships a priority in our lives. That decision was actually made by each of us a long time before we met one another. The commitment to healthy relationships came as a result of seeing the pain and struggle of those about us who hadn't fully appreciated the dimensions of healthy relationships. And it came because we saw that healthy relationships were at the root of the Christian perspective on life.

When we met one another, it didn't take long for us to discover that we had the same values on the subject. Perhaps that is why we were engaged within weeks of our initial introduction, got married five months later, and are still happily married almost twenty-four years later.

Looking back on the path we have traveled together, it is clear to both of us that even though we were committed to it, our relationship did not grow easily. What did it take? Hard work; reaffirmation of priorities on a regular basis; some sacrifice; and a constant quest to understand and know the other person. Like everyone else we have had our great moments and our sour ones. But we can look back and say there have been no regrets.

As we have grown older we have begun to see that there are many different kinds of relationships. There is that of a man and a woman in marriage. There is, of course, that of a parent(s) and child. Beyond that there are the general friendships of varying degrees of intensity that we all pursue and enjoy. Do all of these relationships have anything in common? Absolutely!

And that is what this book is about. As we have wrestled with its contents, we have frequently paused and thanked God for what we have learned, often the hard way through our own failures. And we have learned from many others—our mentors, our friends, and those whom we've tried to serve in our congregation and neighborhood. We owe them a great debt.

This book was written initially as we spent time in solitude at Peace Ledge, our New Hampshire retreat. There in the midst of the New England forest, we sat at the keyboards of a typewriter and a computer. The result of that work is on these pages. Gail would compile the thoughts that came out of our many notebooks, outlines of talks we'd given in the past, and insights that were being generated by our ongoing discussions. Gordon would take the notes and put them in rough draft form. Then would follow the MacDonald version of an editorial conference. The conferences were anything but businesslike; they were marked by hysterical laughter, tears, or expressions of thanks for things we believed came from the Spirit of God working in our hearts and minds. Needless to say, more than one conference ended with hugs and kisses. Then it was back to the keyboards for more drafts and rewriting.

We're grateful to the fine people of the Grace Chapel family in Lexington, Massachusetts, who have encouraged both of us in our ministries. We're appreciative of the assistance of Mr. Philip Rawley of Moody Press, who kept alongside of us as a faithful editor. We're thankful for all of those people who told us that something of this nature on the subject of relationships ought to be written. As some are apt to say in contemporary relationships, "We've taken our best shot," and we believe in what we've said.

1

"We Were Not on That Basis"

Playwright Moss Hart once recalled a childhood Christmas when his father took him shopping, hoping to buy the boy a present he would like. The two walked the New York streets, inspecting the merchandise displayed on scores of pushcarts. Hart's eyes were drawn to chemistry sets and toy printing presses. But the father, a very poor man, had less expensive things in mind.

Each time they would find something the boy wanted, the father would ask the vendor's price, shake his head, and move on. Occasionally he would pick up a smaller, less expensive toy and try to attract his son's attention. But there was no meeting of the minds. Eventually, they came to the end of the line of pushcarts without a purchase.

Hart writes:

> I heard [my father] jingle some coins in his pocket. In a flash I knew it all. He'd gotten together about seventy-five cents to buy me a Christmas present, and he hadn't dared say so in case there was nothing to be had for so small a sum. As I looked up at him I saw a look of despair and disappointment in his eyes that brought me closer to him than I had ever been in my life.
>
> I wanted to throw my arms around him and say, "It doesn't matter. . . . I understand. . . . This is better than a printing press . . . I love you." But instead we stood shivering beside each other for a

1

moment—then turned away from the last two pushcarts and started silently back home. . . . I didn't even take his hand on the way home, nor did he take mine. We were not on that basis. Nor did I ever tell him how close to him I felt that night—that for a little while the concrete wall between father and son had crumbled away and I *knew that we were two lonely people struggling to reach each other.*[1]

The famous advertising slogan has put it simply and well: "Reach out and touch someone." Make contact! Share news; affirm love; renew friendship. To be sure, the phone company that has created this particular message is out to sell us something. And they have done it well. In a thirty-second television spot we are treated to the drama of a daughter calling her mother to announce the birth of a baby, or a run-away son calling to say he'd like to come back home, or two old friends phoning to talk of a shared memory. Who of us hasn't been seized by the powerful ethos of those dramatic encounters? Each time, we are drawn to the exchange by the deep sense of warmth and nostalgia that is there.

Why has that television commercial gripped the hearts of so many Americans? What is there within every one of us that yearns for the intimacy, the joy, and the solidarity expressed by those actors who reach and touch by telephone? Does it symbolize something many of us feel we have never experienced? Does it remind us of past relationships that no longer exist? Are those television dramas finding sympathetic vibrations down deep within the human heart where something says this is the way things ought to be—but aren't?

It is that sort of contact that Moss Hart wished could have happened between himself and his father on the New York street. But, he sadly recounts, "We were not on that basis."

The fact of the matter is that human beings were created to be on that basis. They were made to reach, and they were made to touch and be touched. Thus, when people do not reach and when they are not touched, something indispensable to human health is lost.

Reaching and touching begin as something instinctive. They are the building blocks of relationships. Almost the second a child is born, it begins reaching out for security, nourishment, and warmth. And for a long time it will not stop reaching during virtually every waking moment. In these early moments of human experience, almost all of the reaching is essentially selfish. Nevertheless, reaching is what a baby does best of all. And when it makes contact—the touching—there is obvious peace and serenity. Nowhere is this more beautifully visualized than in the calmness of the moment when the newborn infant reaches for and finds its mother's breast

1. Robert Raines, *A Creative Brooding* (New York: Macmillan, 1977), pp. 45-46.

and draws strength that is far more than the mere physical nourishment of milk.

As the child grows a few months older, it discovers that there are other reasons for reaching. It learns to reach for affection and then for friendship. Some of the reaching will be, unfortunately, too self-centered. There will be increasing reaches for possession and domination. And such reaching, when it happens, can become ugly and distasteful. What was once beautiful becomes a sign of unrestrained selfishness, and, unless disciplined, it leads to destructiveness.

All the way into normal adolescence there will be a constant rhythm of reaching: establishing oneself in a matrix of relationships from family, to peer group, to the larger world of the generations. But as maturity occurs, it is hoped the reaching will also become the reaching of giving and sharing. For that is one of the great objectives of human growth—the movement of life from reaching only for oneself to reaching for the sake of others. That process of maturation may be the most important single matter of personal growth and development that there is. To the extent that it does not happen, we have wars, crime, exploitation, and unresolved human conflict.

Generally speaking, everyone reaches, but not everyone touches. As we said before, reaching is instinctive; but for the most part *touching is learned.* For in touching we give *and* receive, talk *and* listen, share ourselves *and* see into another. And not everyone can do that or will do it.

In the most literal sense of the word, we all need to be touched. Edmund Janss writes:

> On St. Thomas Mount in Madras, India, I once watched a housemother tenderly holding a baby. She was feeding her while humming a gentle song. The baby had been found on a trash heap crying weakly. I asked the houseparent about her feeding method. She nodded and said, "If we don't hold them and sing to them while we feed them, they often die."[2]

Those babies are not unique. As we learn more and more about the human being we discover that being touched in all sorts of ways is basic to health and perhaps even human survival. William Glasser, author of *Reality Therapy,* suggests that "psychiatry must be concerned with two basic psychological needs: 1) the need to love and be loved and, 2) the need to feel that we are worthwhile to ourselves and others."[3]

2. Edmund Janss, *How to Give Your Children Everything They Really Need* (Wheaton, Ill.: Tyndale, 1979), p. 29.
3. William Glasser, *Reality Therapy: A New Approach to Psychiatry* (New York: Harper & Row, 1975), p. 9.

In his book *The Hurried Child*, David Elkind points out that as early as the cradle days, the social and spiritual adjustments of an adolescent may be determined. Children long to be held, mothered, thanked, and consulted, he claims, and if those basic needs are unmet so that the child does not feel "heard," feelings of anger and rebellion are stored up that will most likely be released during the teen years. Like it or not, our touch or lack of touch affects others drastically.[4]

But that is not all. James J. Lynch, a leading specialist in psychosomatic medicine at the University of Maryland, argues that social isolation brings emotional and then *physical deterioration*. Disease, he suggests, can be "loneliness induced." Lynch stresses the importance of the family and of caring relationships for friends and neighbors. "Simply put there is a biological basis for our need to form human relationships. If we fail to fulfill that need, our health is in peril."[5]

The poet W. H. Auden said, "We must love one another or die."

The thoughts of these experts fit perfectly with Scripture's explanations of men and women and their relationships to God and to one another. In the earliest paragraphs of the Bible, God, surveying the work of creation, looked upon the first man and said, "It is not good for man to be alone."

Here was the initial version of humankind in what we can only call a perfect setting. There was an absence of disease, of terror, and of other elements hostile to his survival. But merely being a beautiful, tranquil setting was inadequate. *He was alone!* And, according to the Creator, "It is not good."

Yet in spite of the biblical observation and in spite of an increasing number of claims that the quality of one's relationships is a key to holistic (whole person) health, we live in a day where—in spite of all the reaching—little touching is really happening.

In light of all the technology of the past seventy-five years that has made it possible for people to communicate instantly or to travel great distances in short time spans to be with one another, it is ironic that evidence seems to indicate that less touching is going on now than a generation ago.

Although our accumulation of knowledge has helped us to understand the workings of the human mind, the emotions, and the effect of past experiences, which make us much of what we are, we seem actually to be able to touch each other less than ever before.

4. David Elkind, *The Hurried Child* (Reading, Mass.: Addison-Wesley, 1981), p. 190.
5. James J. Lynch, *The Broken Heart: The Medical Consequences of Loneliness* (New York: Basic Books, 1979).

In marital relationships (the most intensive of all human relationships) the divorce rate continues to soar, suggesting that while people as a rule may be more educated, more highly skilled, and more richly experienced, they have not learned how to maintain satisfactory relationships amid the pressures of contemporary life. A recent article in the Boston *Globe* reports that a Dallas lawyer, Averil Schweitzer, arranged for a mass dissolution of 108 marriages at one divorce hearing. Family court judge Linda Thomas convened the group in an auditorium, asked them all to rise and swear in unison that their papers were truthful, and then said, "I grant your divorce per your decree." The entire session lasted twenty minutes.

Some so-called avant-garde thinkers in our society have suggested that marriage as a relational institution is a thing of the past. But it is obvious now that no other relational structure has come along to take its place and provide the necessary nurture most people seek. The result? As a society, we are lonelier than ever.

The reaches and touches within the North American family apparently leave something to be desired in many homes, if the increasing number of run-aways, the growing drug problem, and the upsurge of teenage suicides are any indication.

The court dockets of our nation are jammed with cases of people suing one another. The anger one observes between drivers in a traffic jam, the intensive competition in many businesses that leads to unethical and immoral activities, and the general complaint among middle-aged men that they have few if any close friends are all signs of a diminution of relationships that include both reaching and touching. Add to these the international tragedies of racism, war, and violence, and it becomes easy to conclude that healthy human relationships such as we were created to enjoy are indeed a rare commodity.

Perhaps it is important to say that when someone takes a hard look at the present scene and notes the evidences of broken relationships, that is not to suggest that there was a time in our history when things were significantly better. We need not try to look backward with nostalgia to some "better day." Perhaps there has been no "better day." What is important, however, about this time in which we live is the fact that humanity can claim advances of a kind in so many other areas of reality.

While we have leaped ahead in science and technology, while we understand through research so much about the human brain as well as the body, and while we have accumulated vast reservoirs of knowledge about almost everything, we apparently have made virtually no progress in the area of how people are brought together to reach and touch—the core of the human experience.

Nations glare at each other, fingers on the nuclear buttons. Races have made relatively little advance in crossing over into understanding and tolerance. Individuals *seem* more angry, competitive, and exploitive than ever. Why has there been so much advance in every part of life except in that of relationships? Why is Moss Hart's inability to grab the hand of his father in a melancholy moment so symbolic of where the world is today? Perhaps the best thing we can say about the state of contemporary human relationships is that at least we have not yet destroyed the entire human race in one gigantic act of suicide.

Christians affirm the Bible as the Word of God. On its pages are found eternal truths that provide all we need to know about God's design for life—existence as He meant it to be. At its very center, the Bible is a book about relationships: what they were meant to be, what shatters them, and what brings about reconciliation. There is no better treatment of the subject of relationships than what is found in the Scriptures. The principles there have endured through the centuries and are as relevant today as they were the day they were written down.

No one in the Scriptures said more about relationships than Jesus Christ. In the hours just before He was taken captive in the Garden of Gethsemane, for example, He spoke to His disciples about many important matters, relationships among them. When you read the account of that conversation, you get the feeling that it was a summation of the discipleship process: a quick recap of the most significant things He had taught them over the preceding three years. The matters He was raising were the issues that He wanted planted deepest and yet most visibly in their lives.

Among those subjects? The disciples' courage, their spiritual energy, their faithfulness to His commandments. And then something else: *their relationships.* He talked of reaching and touching. The apostle John gives us what must have been a synopsis of the talk, and when he comes to what Jesus said about relationships, he quotes Him like this:

> A new commandment I give to you, that you love one another, even as I have loved you, that you also love one another. By this all men will know that you are my disciples, if you have love for one another. (John 13:34-35, RSV*)

*Revised Standard Version.

In those comments of Christ's, we have a thoroughly adequate outline of the Bible's teaching on what it means to reach out and touch. *It seems to be His chief concern for them.* The language is dramatic: "new commandment. . . ," "as I have loved. . . ," "all men. . . ." And it is dramatic because He obviously wanted them to be reaching *and* touching men, and if that would happen, everyone, He proposed, would take note that they were His disciples, first-class dependable productions of His gospel. By reaching and touching one another first, they would be able to reach and touch the world.

It ought not to surprise us that Jesus had to talk about relationships to these twelve men, for the subject had not come automatically into the priorities of their thinking or performance.

A quick look over the three-year history of their time with Christ offers insights concerning their relational blind spots. There had been ideological rivalries; there had been suggestions of competition for whatever they thought to be first place in the small but burgeoning movement; there had been concerns about who would be remembered as the greatest among them; there had been moments of volatile anger and outrage such as on the day a few of them wanted to bring fire (as if they could) down upon a village for refusing them hospitality. They frequently demonstrated insensitivity toward suffering and poverty; and later on that very evening they would illustrate that their courage to stand with the Lord was quite limited and, given a chance, would melt rather quickly.

The fact is that the disciples, like so many around them, were well-meaning men, but they tended to be relationally incompetent. And 2000 years later, times have not dramatically changed.

John's quotation of Jesus' teaching on relationships breaks into an interesting three-point outline. The first stunning point lies in the fact that *Christ commands His disciples to love one another.* He makes plain that He is not suggesting some nice idea or expressing a wistful, sentimental thought. They were to *choose* to love one another in response to His commandment as master discipler.

Second in the outline, Jesus' command was not an ambiguous notion. The twelve were to love one another in the same way they'd been loved by Him. To use the language of this book, they were to reach as He had reached and touch as He had touched them. They had at their disposal a living Model of three years of relationship, which had been indelibly stamped into their souls.

Finally, if they would do that, a witness of startling proportions would be established. In their relationships was the authentication of witness.

Followers of Christ would be marked, first and foremost, by *love for one another and for the world.* Their reach and their touch would be revolutionary, unique, and powerful. And wherever this reaching and touching happened, humanity did indeed take note and was strangely drawn. What did they see?

They saw compassion: people placing at one another's disposal any necessary resource in a time of trouble—money, food, shelter, even the laying down of life. *They saw new kinds of friendships:* the older and the younger drawing strength from one another; the strong and the weaker supporting and leaning upon one another. *They saw a new kind of organization:* people working together for the common objectives of world evangelization. *They saw new families and marriages:* men and women treating each other with dignity, respect, and servanthood; children stamped with special value and esteem. *They saw new sorts of relationships in businesses:* masters treating servants as brothers; employees giving their employers a new level of productivity; those entering into contract keeping their word. The evidence of genuine discipleship in Christian relationships was simply unimpeachable.

The Christian community has often spoken of the Great Commission, that of going into the world to proclaim the love of Jesus Christ. But it may be important to note that this *great commandment* has to *precede* the Great Commission. People who have never learned to love one another can hardly tell the rest of the world of the love of Christ.

So it all begins with a new (or great) commandment. Why new? And why a commandment? In a sense, the commandment was not new; it had simply been forgotten. The kind of love that Christ was highlighting for the disciples was actually as old as creation itself. It was the love out of which God created the heavens and the earth, by which He chose to make man and woman so that He could enjoy fellowship with them.

And it was the love of which John would write when he said that God so loved the world that He gave His only Son. No, the commandment was new only in the sense that it focused on a quality of relationship that had for the most part been forgotten through the centuries. What should have been Christlike love in relationships had degenerated into legalism, competition, and exploitation. There was little of the love of the new commandment.

In the time when Jesus stated this "new" (but actually very old) commandment, men had to be told stories like the one featuring the Good Samaritan. Apparently no one was shocked at the description of a priest or a Levite who would pass a dying man at the roadside because he had other priorities to which he had to give attention. A religious fervor of a frightening brand had so blinded certain kinds of people that they did not hear what they were actually saying when they criticized Jesus for showing compassion to an immoral woman who was weeping for her sins. It was a time in which relationships were calloused, competitive, marked with suspicion. We ought not to ignore this ancient state of affairs; it can easily be repeated in any generation. And some would say that it is apparent in sectors of the Christian church today.

So Jesus had to commend the disciples to this sort of special love because He knew that what He was calling them to was not popular, natural, or instinctive. It was a form of relationship not known then or now among ordinary people. There have always been substitutes for it, which tend to be cheap and inadequate. But the love of which Christ spoke is something done by choice. It has never flowed naturally out of a human heart where the spiritual disease of sin has been in control.

This love that Christ commended to the disciples as the only legitimate way of reaching and touching has been unnatural ever since the tragedy in the lives of the first two human beings, Adam and Eve.

We know few details about the relationship of the first man and woman in the Garden of Eden except that there appears to have been an unlimited experience of communication and companionship between the two of them as they set out to implement the mandate of the Creator to be fruitful and multiply, to explore or subdue the earth and have dominion over it. How long a period of time they lived in this experience of what Moses would later call "one flesh" is unknown.

What is known, however, is that the first man and woman made an unfortunate series of choices in response to temptations from the serpent. And having disobeyed the commandments of God, the devastating result was *the shattering of all levels of their once-healthy relationships.*

First, there was immediate *estrangement from God* with whom they had normally enjoyed daily communion. When God came searching for them, the Scriptures indicate that they were hiding, ashamed of their choices, strangely embarrassed over their naked appearance. It was apparent that for the first time they had something unfortunate to hide, a secret they would have wished to keep from God. And that seriously diminished their relationship with Him.

In Genesis 3 we are told that when God entered the Garden that day to seek (you could say to reach and touch) Adam and Eve, they were nowhere to be found. It is almost humorous to imagine Adam off in the bushes hoping that God would not find him. What had previously been a beautiful fellowship was now something to be avoided. Adam and Eve were embarrassed. They'd tried what they thought was a better way, and now they didn't want to have to account for its effects. So they hid. And humankind has tended to hide from God ever since. But still He comes in search of us; God is always seizing the initiative.

It is also obvious that a *second relationship was shattered, that of Adam to himself; of Eve to herself.* Part of Adam was at war with another part, and he was no longer pleased with himself. Now there was something for which an excuse had to be manufactured. Made to be a fully integrated human being, Adam now was multiple in his parts, and one part of him had betrayed another part. The whole man once created was not whole any longer.

The tragic decentralization of a once-whole person is seen again and again in our inconsistent behaviors. A person's mind, for example, can intellectually agree with the data that says cigarette smoking causes cancer. But another part of that same person will crave the narcotic effect of the tobacco and, in conflict with the intellect, choose to smoke. We can tell ourselves (intellectually) that it is prudent to attach our safety belts but ignore that fact all the same because using them is inconvenient or uncomfortable. Such inconsistency is among the examples of how people can be out of touch with themselves.

Because of disobedience *the third relationship*—that of Adam and Eve with one another—was shattered also. The Bible says that they began to blame one another. Adam refused to accept responsibility for his own actions. And when he put the blame upon Eve, Adam was suggesting that she was something less of a person than he, that he could have got along without her just fine. What a far cry from the grateful man who, when seeing Eve for the first time, had cried out, "At last; this is bone of my bone, flesh of my flesh." But now in a sudden moment of defensiveness and resistance to repentance, Adam displayed for all humanity the proud heart that blames others for the consequences of deeds and attitudes. Adam and Eve's once intimate relationship no longer existed.

Today we inherit that same attitude, and the evidence of it becomes apparent every time a person refuses to face accountability for his/her own actions. Each time we blame our failures upon the actions of others, the chances are we are simply repeating the same error Adam made when he backed off from Eve in an attempt to vindicate himself.

Adam and Eve also forfeited *the privilege of a fourth kind of relationship* because of their disobedience to God. It was that of *their touch with all of nature about them.* Before sin entered the world, man enjoyed dominion over nature. His work was the task of discovery and appreciation of what God had placed there to reflect His own glory. But no longer would that be true. "Now," God told them, "you will have to wrestle with nature for whatever you get out of it. It will no longer obediently respond to your command."

The evidence of man's estrangement from the earth is in abundant in our lack of respect for nature. As a people we have exploited the earth, draining it of its assets, spoiling much of its beauty, and littering it with our toxins, our nuclear wastes, and our garbage. In the vivid imagery of pollution is a picture not only of what we've done to creation, but of what we have so often done to one another.

There is a biblical suggestion of a *fifth shattered relationship,* and that would be found in creation itself. All of nature was somehow touched by Adam and Eve's sin, an evidence of the explosive and poisonous quality of sin's power. As a result, nature would no longer fully reflect the glory of the Creator as it had been designed to do. From that time forth everything man would touch would be strangely stained, losing its reflective quality. So serious a matter was this that Paul would later suggest that all of creation awaits, even cries out, for the redemption of the children of God, for only then will creation be restored to its original condition: that of reflecting the glory and majesty of God.

When Adam and Eve disobeyed God, creation became, for all practical purposes, a loveless place. Never again would the quality of relationships once enjoyed in the Garden be seen in such brilliance until Jesus Christ would come into the shattered world, bringing a new burst of the love that had once characterized time and space. And it was this kind of love that He wanted the disciples to be careful to implement in their relationships with one another. The oneness of relationships originally experienced in the Garden was the oneness Jesus desired for the disciples.

Today all of us struggle in our reaching and touching because of those shattered relationships. We were made to enjoy that sort of oneness with God, ourselves, with one another, and our world. But much of what we were made for simply isn't working.

And without that oneness of love in relationships, we become like a modern battery-driven toy or tool that is running low on power. It has great capacity to function, but because the power is strictly limited, the performance too is tragically limited.

One is reminded of the small girl who had found scissors and proceeded to cut off some of her hair. When her mother looked in and saw what had happened, she cried, "Mary, what have you done to your hair?" And little Mary responded, "How did you know, Mommy? I tried to hide it in the wastebasket."

We may try to hide the fact that relationships in this modern world are not doing well. We can sing about relationships; we can lecture and preach about them; we can attempt to celebrate relationships as being something more than they are; but it is quite obvious to anyone that humanity has cut off its hair, and the consequences cannot be hidden.

When Jesus Christ gave the disciples His commandment, He was calling them to an effectual repudiation of broken relationships and to an embracing of a new quality of oneness with one another. He knew that the contagion of it would be tremendous, and so it was.

It is sad to think of a young boy like Moss Hart wanting to reach out to his father and take his hand. What reassurance and what affection could have passed between father and son. But it didn't happen, and the loneliness of two people went unhealed. "We were not on that basis," Hart recalls.

Life takes on new color when some of us do get on that basis. Understanding what it means not only to reach but also to touch, we begin to develop new relationships of varying intensities. And when we move to that "basis," the world learns something about genuine Christianity.

The sorts of relationships in marriage, family, and friendships that reflect the kind of love Christ was talking about are built upon five building blocks. The first is what we're going to call *commitment*—the choice the persons in a relationship make to give themselves to one another. It is in some kind of commitment that all reaching and touching begins.

Transparency—the ability of any one of us to open his/her life up to others—is the second of the blocks. To the extent that one resists transparency, or openness, a relationship becomes strictly limited and of diminished effectiveness.

We intend to call the third building block *sensitivity*, because it would seem that a relationship demands the ability of those involved to discover what is in the other person. These three blocks point toward a fourth, that of *communication* in which people share their perspectives and perplexities. And if these four blocks have been properly arranged, there will be the beauty of a fifth, something we've chosen to call *enablement*. Here it is that people build in each other's lives causing opportunities for wholeness and growth. And that is the chief objective of all relationships, at least the kind of which Jesus Christ was speaking with His disciples.

When such relationships are in force, the world not only takes note of genuine disciples, but the world enjoys a bit more peace and tranquility, something God wills for it to have.

2

Breathe!

Nelson Pendergrass, an Oklahoma rancher, once made a coura-geous commitment to another person. The commitment was made the day that he, along with his wife and two sons, invited David, a sixteen-year-old boy, to come and live in his home. Repeatedly Da-vid had been in trouble with the law, and the expectation was that the brand of love practiced in the Pendergrass home would melt what seemed to have become a very hard juvenile heart. "I thought I was the kind of man that could help him change," Pendergrass later wrote.[1]

But it didn't seem to work. David did not respond to the relational climate of the Pendergrass home or any attempt to cross over into his life. In fact he appeared, if anything, to grow more resistant to relationships than ever. Things became so bad that Nelson Pender-grass began to seriously consider the possibility that he had failed and that David would have to be returned to juvenile court. It was a terrible decision, and each day the possibility that it would have to be made came closer.

Then Nelson had a serious ranching accident that sent him to the intensive care unit of the local hospital. While there recovering from his injuries, a blood clot suddenly entered his heart. In a matter of minutes Pendergrass was fighting for his life. Later he would admit

1. "Our Blue-eyed Maverick," *Guideposts*, November 1982, pp. 24-29.

that the pain in those moments was so great that he had to fight the temptation to give up and welcome death as a relief. What kept him going?

It was a nurse that made the difference. He writes, "I gasped for air. But it hurt too much to breathe. Better to just drift away, I told myself. Away from the fear, from the pain, forever.

"But there was the nurse, her face not six inches from mine. 'Breathe. You've got to breathe,' she said.

"Leave me alone, I wanted to scream. Let me die. But no, she was still there. 'Breathe,' she said, 'Breathe . . . breathe . . . breathe.' *I was willing to give up, but she was not.* Again and again, I fought to take a breath as she called to me."[2]

Nelson Pendergrass made it through the crisis that day, but the thanks, he says, belongs to that nurse who insisted that he keep on breathing when he wanted to quit.

Not many days afterward the powerful lesson of those terrible moments when he had wanted to die came home to the rancher's heart. Nelson began to connect the experience in the intensive care unit with what was going on back at the ranch with David, the unresponsive teenager. Pendergrass had come close to sending the boy back to the juvenile court. David showed no evidence of caring what happened to himself; so why should anyone else care?

But when it came to David's situation, wasn't he, Nelson asked himself, in the same position as the nurse in the ICU who had coaxed and prodded him back to life? Wasn't it his turn to confront this boy and shout the equivalent of "Breathe!" That blunt question caused the foster-father to postpone his decision and give David another chance.

Then one night when the relationship between Nelson and David seemed to reach a peak of stress, Nelson found a way to apply the lesson he'd so painfully learned. David had been arrested for stealing a car, and Pendergrass had to go to the police station to face him. When they met in the holding cell, David's first reaction was to tell Nelson to leave him alone, that he didn't care any longer. But Nelson, remembering his own experience with the nurse, told David that he found that notion unacceptable.

"David," he said to the boy, "as long as you're under my supervision, you're not giving up on life. And I'm not giving up on you either. We're not quitting. You're coming home. And you and I and the Lord are going to get through all of this."

The crisis passed, and as the months went by Nelson Pendergrass

2. Ibid.

and his foster son, David, forged a new relationship. Today David is a young husband and father. But it has all come to pass because one man made a commitment to teach another how to "breathe."

When Jesus called upon His disciples to love one another, He did not offer empty words. In effect He was commanding that they "breathe" in a relationally polluted world. Lest they make any mistake about the nature of the relationship He had in mind, He provided an object lesson. "Love one another," He said, "as I have loved you." Or, "Reach and touch just as I have reached out and touched you."

It is probable that John, the writer, does not offer the complete text of Jesus' words. Had he done so we might learn that Jesus carefully reviewed some moments in His relationship with the disciples in which His love had been demonstrated. At any rate, if we can learn something of the way Christ loved those disciples, then we might understand how He desires those who follow Him, then and now, to relate to one another. It would also seem logical, and this is important, that the principles of His love would fit all relationships: friendships, teaching or discipling relationships, Christian work relationships, families, and marriages.

Later in New Testament times, Paul would struggle to find an adequate model of marital love for Ephesian men. In that case he was writing to people who knew almost nothing about the kind of love that characterizes Christian disciples. His answer to that problem of teaching the meaning of love was to seize upon the form of Christ's love for the church:

> Husbands, love your wives, as Christ loved the church and *gave himself* for her, that he *might sanctify her,* having cleansed her by the washing of water with the word, that he *might present the church to himself in splendor,* without spot or wrinkle or any such thing, that she might be holy and without blemish. (Ephesians 5:25-27, RSV: italics added)

Thus, the old apostle highlighted three ways in which that love had become visible. First, he wrote, Christ gave Himself (in death) for the church. Second, He sanctified the church. In that sense Jesus is in the process of purifying and perfecting the church, giving it the gifts and powers it needs. Finally, Christ will present the church to Himself as His prized possession, His Bride, when it has been brought to maturity.

John does not give us the same sort of outline or detail that Paul does in that beautiful passage on Christian marriage. Therefore we are left to trace back across the life and work of Jesus in relationship to His disciples to ask again, How did He love them anyway?

It seems obvious that the first of many possible answers is this: *Jesus committed Himself to them,* just as Nelson Pendergrass committed himself to a juvenile delinquent who desperately needed the kind of love that changes a life.

In effect that commitment began to form when Jesus Christ accepted the mandate of the heavenly Father to leave heaven and become the God-man, living for thirty-three years in the world. Paul talks about this remarkable decision in Philippians, chapter 2, when he says that Christ voluntarily "emptied" Himself of His rights as the prince of heaven for a time in order to commit Himself to a relationship with human beings who would follow Him. It was a commitment we desperately needed, because without it humankind was destined to live on a divergent track away from the eternal blessings of God. As someone has written:

> Because we children of Adam want
> to become great,
> He became small.
> Because we will not stoop,
> He humbled himself.
> Because we want to rule,
> He came to serve.

The commitment Jesus made to His disciples came about first as He discovered each man and invited him to join Him. "Follow me," He said to Peter and the others, "and I will make you fishers of men" (Mark 1:17). It was His way of reaching into their worlds and proposing a relationship. "You follow, and I will commit to providing an opportunity for you to grow to become everything your Heavenly Father created you to be."

There is significance in this order of things. Before the disciples could commit to Christ, He committed to each of them. God the Father showed this same pattern, according to Paul, when He showed His love toward us while we were yet sinners (see Romans 5:8). Christ's brand of love commits before there is a promise of response. And that commitment offers a relationship that eventuates in growth and maturity.

Later Jesus would ask the disciples to continue the pattern of that same commitment in their reaching and touching of one another and, obviously, beyond themselves to whomever they would encounter.

It is this principle of commitment that lies at the beginning of every relationship circumscribed by love. Whether we are talking of the relationship of marriage, that of a mentor to a follower, or that of two people who have chosen to be friends, there is at the beginning of their walk together a choice to be made—a commitment that says, "Your growth and development are my ultimate aim in this encounter as long as it is supposed to last."

All relationships of value begin with a commitment of some kind. And sometimes when stress hits its peak in any relationship, it is only the commitment that keeps it together.

GAIL: I can't get out of my mind an uproarious experience when our son, Mark, went to get his first driver's license. As in every American home, it was a big day for Mark as well as for his nervous parents. Unfortunately, when the time came to leave for the agency where new drivers are tested, Gordon was nowhere to be found, and he had our car. (Later we learned that he'd got his signals mixed and didn't know the time sequence). So Mark and I frantically ran to our second vehicle, a pickup truck, and headed for what we in Massachusetts call the "Registry." Everything went wrong. We missed a key turn on the way; it appeared as if the registration in the truck was out of date, meaning that the vehicle was unusable; and finally—when we did locate the right registration—that the truck was about the most inconvenient sort of transportation for a driver's test. The inspector told us that the law required that Mark would have to do the driving, that the inspector would have to sit in the cab, and that I (believe it or not) would have to ride in the open bed of the back of the truck. Me, with my dress and heels. I thought he was kidding, but bureaucrat that he was, he wasn't.

I heard myself saying to him, "Sir, if it means that my son can be licensed, I'm glad to sit in the bed of the truck. We're committed to each other." And I assumed my position. The inspector was charmed. As we started out of the parking lot, I remember thinking, *This is what commitment is all about—enormous inconvenience at times for the good of someone else. Mark will learn from his mother's understanding of the term.* And he did. None of us ever forgot the day we learned something more about the meaning of commitment to each other.

When Jesus gave His disciples the new commandment that they ought to love one another, the first implication of His directive was that they would have to make a commitment to each other.

A commitment is a necessity when there is something that has to be corrected or overcome, when a deliberate choice has to be made to do or be something that one would not otherwise choose to do. In this case the thing that had to be overcome was in the basic nature of each of the twelve: selfishness, or self-centeredness. And that is in the nature of every human being. That's why we have to make commitments.

To love in accordance with Christ's commandment, one must actually *overcome* basic human nature. For Christ's view of love involves giving and serving. By contrast, human nature's brand of love involves receiving and dominating.

We will never understand Christian love until we begin with the assumption that there is a spiritual repellent within each of us. We like to reach but not necessarily to touch. We like to be touched but not necessarily at the expense of reaching. Christ was commanding that the disciples do both.

Their commitment to one another would have to be a deliberate choice to love each other. It would not be made on the basis of personal attractiveness, common interests (apart from their call in Christ), or similar backgrounds. The fact of the matter was that in all three areas the disciples shared virtually none of those ingredients. To love one another had already proved on occasion to be hard work. So if there was to be love, it would have to be by choice.

We have seen this principle of commitment at work in scores of situations. But one that stands out is seen in the family of Charlie and Linda Austin. Charlie is a highly respected news reporter on Boston television. He and Linda have three wonderful children, the youngest of which is Danielle, a Down's syndrome child who is presently eight years of age. When Danielle was born, the medical experts urged Charlie and Linda to institutionalize Danielle and pursue a normal life for themselves. But the couple made a commitment, to Danielle and to each other. As long as it was possible, Danielle would live at home and grow and learn to the full extent of her potential.

As time passed, Danielle had a number of physical crises during which everyone was sure she would die. But each time God spared her life, and she became more and more an object of the family's love. But not their's only. People in our congregation fell in love with Danielle, and before long she was a part of a special education Sunday school class at Grace Chapel. Soon she was singing, responding to stories about Christ, and becoming an important part of a social unit. Everyone grew because of Danielle and grew in a way that would probably not have happened if Danielle had been what we call a normal child. No one knows how long Danielle will remain in the Austin home or when she will be called to God's home, because Down's syndrome children do not have long life expectancies. But eight years have passed now, and she continues to be the light of many lives. It all began because four special people, Charlie, Linda Austin, and their other two daughters, Lisa and Amy, saw that relationships begin with a commitment even when the way is hard and the destination difficult to define.

A romantic view of love suggests that we *fall in love*. It supposes that love is something that happens to people while they are in a passive state. Christian love, however, begins with a commandment that calls us to choose to love people regardless of their human attractiveness. It is active; not passive.

Love of this sort was first demonstrated in the heavenly Father when He came searching for disobedient children. Adam fled; God came searching. Later that search would be illustrated in the beautiful picture of the shepherd seeking a lost lamb. Jesus would picture that love in the father of the prodigal son, who was seen standing, waiting for his son's return.

In each case, there is the message of one who loves and searches and another who is unlovely but loved nevertheless. The one who loves is committed to the relationship even if the one who is loved has broken all of the boundaries of the relationship.

That kind of love is seen not only in the search but in the role the lover voluntarily accepts in the relationship. It is the role of a servant. And Christ most powerfully illustrated servanthood when He gathered His disciples and washed their feet as only the lowest of servants might have been willing to do. The disciples were shocked at the time, especially Peter. But when He'd finished that stunning demonstration of servanthood, He instructed the disciples to do the same in principle for one another.

> GAIL: Whenever I go back to that dramatic foot-washing scene and think about what happened there, I can't get Judas Iscariot out of my mind. He was there, and when Jesus knelt to wash his feet, He knew what was about to happen. Jesus really deserved a lot better from Judas. He didn't get it, and He knew he wasn't going to get it. But still He served him because He was committed

> to the end to serve Judas. It's a solid lesson to me every time I'm tempted to cut off someone because I feel he has betrayed me.

Serving is a rather unpopular element in any relationship but that of the Christian kind. Our culture teaches us to pursue a brand of kingship, not servanthood. We are taught to dominate rather than defer. We are taught to take rather than give.

To serve is to ask the growth question: What do others in this relationship need that I can give that will enhance their growth?

The missionary leader D. E. Hoste, who was successor to J. Hudson Taylor, understood servanthood, and he carried a great personal vision of the development of Chinese Christians as leaders in their own churches. He wrote: "Pray that the missionaries may have the grace and wisdom to make the most of their Chinese fellow workers, not to stunt them or stand in their way but to help and strengthen them."[3]

That is servanthood in its most practical sense. And Hoste spent his life committed to the Chinese Christians. For him commitment meant servanthood. If Hoste was a great leader it was because he acted out the *Living Bible* paraphrase of Luke 9:48: "Your care for others is the measure of your greatness."

There was a memorable moment in the life of Moses when he began to face squarely the fact that he would never enter into the Promised Land with the people he had led for forty years. He pled with God for the privilege of moving ahead with the people and was refused. But it is important to note what God did ask Moses to do: "Commission Joshua to replace you, and then encourage him, for he shall lead the people across to conquer the land you will see from the mountain top (Deuteronomy 3:28, TLB*).

Make a commitment, Moses; surrender your own rights. Put another in your place, and make sure that he is effective and successful. That is what God was asking Moses to do, and it is the essence of Christian relationships.

Arnold Parker has told the story of a nurse named Hulda. Her pastor, Parker writes, noted that she was marked with bruises and scratches one day when she came to church. And because she did not volunteer information as to what had happened, he inquired of another nurse who worked with Hulda.

The Living Bible.

3. Phyllis Thompson, *D. E. Hoste: A Prince with God* (London: Lutterworth, n.d.), p. 107.

Two weeks previously, a little fourteen year old girl had been brought into the hospital, violently insane. A day or so later the physician in charge of that section told her story at the daily staff meeting. The little girl had been reared in abject poverty. Her father and mother were both alcoholics. Never in her entire life had she been made to feel wanted and needed. Never had she known what kindness and affection were. One day at the age of twelve she had watched as her drunken mother and father, in a violent argument, struggled for possession of a shotgun. She had seen the gun fire and watched as the life of her father ended on the floor. The mother was charged with manslaughter and paroled, presumably to care for the child. But in the next two years the same old life continued and all she knew from her mother were curses and beatings. Finally her little mind became so filled with hatred and resentment towards all human beings it rejected reality and snapped. She drifted off into fantasy and delusion and became violently insane.

The physician then told the staff that a part of her therapy must be catharsis. She must be allowed to vent her wrath on someone, to spew out some of the pent-up hatred which had poisoned her so. The physician then called for volunteers. Hulda raised her hand.

Then for one hour a day for two weeks Hulda went into the cell with this demented girl and allowed her to have her catharsis. She took all of her kicks, all of her pounding, all of her clawing and scratching until the girls' strength was spent and she crouched in a corner, trembling like a frightened, trapped little animal. Then, as Hulda left the cell, each day she would pause at the door, turn and face the girl. And there with her own blood streaming down her face she would smile at the girl and repeat these words, "Darling—I love you! Darling—I love you."[4]

That is commitment—commitment to serve. And it was done in the midst of great pain and sacrifice. Sometimes commitment is like that.

To serve in Christ's view of things is not to pick out the most easily served or the most likeable. It is a commitment that does not judge people in the human framework but rather sees people as Christ saw them: as valuable in the sight of the Father.

To serve is to lay aside one's rights. And that is what Jesus was asking the twelve to do—to lay aside their personal rights and claims and ask how the interests of others could be addressed. Remember that the disciples did not own a good record in the area of surrendering personal rights. Rights were very much on their minds. Now Jesus was asking in effect that they switch their priorities from their own rights to the rights of their brothers.

4. Arnold Parker, *Release from Phoniness* (Waco, Tex.: Word, 1969), pp. 76-78.

When Jesus found the twelve one by one at the shore, in the business office, and in crowds, they were rough, crude, generally unlikeable people. None were men that most of us would have picked. But He saw possibility in them, and He made a commitment.

"Breathe!" He said, when they thought they were worthless and too sinful. "Breathe!" He said, when they had failed miserably in doing the simplest things. "Breathe!" He said, when their faith was so small that they panicked in the middle of a storm. His commitment was to keep them breathing.

> GAIL: Commitment to serve can indeed be dramatic or painful. I hope we can remember, however, that commitment can be lots and lots of fun—especially when the other person responds. I have the privilege of being part of almost 50 women who meet every Tuesday morning and train to teach 400 other women in Bible study. We're committed to each other, and the price of our commitment is high. But anyone who entered into our fellowship each week would find almost no trace whatsoever of heaviness or drudgery. We have fun, and we're growing in our lives together. But the excitement springs from an initial commitment to serve each other.

Preacher Charles Spurgeon likened Christ's commitment to His disciples to the concern of the camper who has but one match left with which to start a fire. As a tiny flicker of flame grows, the camper watches and guards it intently, feeding it enough fuel to keep growing but not so much that it will be smothered. Our Lord did that for men and women who represented the smallest spark of faith, Spurgeon said. He nursed the spark in anticipation of a fire in the future.

"Breathe!" we say to one another, when we make a commitment to someone else in a relationship. That was how a nurse kept Nelson Pendergrass alive and what he learned to do to keep a young boy alive who wanted to quit. And it was what Jesus Christ wanted the disciples to do for one another when life and work became so tough that each one would be tempted to want to quit.

A man and woman who enter into marriage are promising to keep each other "breathing" and therefore growing. Two friends who begin to support one another have made a commitment to keep one another "breathing." An older man or woman who accepts mentoring responsibility for a younger has promised to keep the other "breathing." This is where relationships begin: a promise made that *no matter what, we will keep each other breathing.* And we're not going to stop! That's commitment.

3

Open Windows

An architect is said to have once offered to construct a house for the philosopher Plato, and, assuming that Plato was interested in total privacy, he pledged that the house would be designed in such a way that no one would be able to see into any of its rooms from the outside.

But Plato responded, "I will give you twice as much if you build a house for me so that everyone can see into every room."

Plato had no problem with transparency. He believed that if one has nothing to hide and if, by contrast, one has lots of life to share, then the objective may be to enlarge the windows rather than to expand the walls. All of this is illustrative of an issue we'd like to call *transparency.* Increasingly it becomes clear that transparency is a significant element in the pursuit of healthy human relationships. It cannot be overlooked or ignored.

The principle of transparency focuses on the question of how much we will permit others to know about us. We could call it "knowability." That of course would be the opposite of "unknowability," and to the extent that any of us is "unknowable," the quality of our relationships will suffer.

Some people want to be widely known, but for questionable reasons. It is not that they are pursuing relational closeness or intimacy but rather that they seek popularity, recognition, or a following that will help them reach an objective. That objective can be financial profit, applause, power, or even a strange sort of personal acceptance that one thinks he needs.

Because of these people there is a large industry that has as its primary product the enlargement of one's knowability. Sometimes it is called the "recognition factor." Public relations firms make large amounts of money creating what they call "public images" for politicians, entertainers, and athletes—anyone who wants to be widely known for the purpose of making a living. These firms produce and plant press releases, develop carefully written biographies, seek magazine interviews, and guarantee that flattering stories will be subtly "leaked" in order to trigger public curiosity about people. All of it is done to make a client "knowable" or recognizable but always and only on the client's terms. Conversely, those things a person does not want known are just as carefully managed so that the public is kept in ignorance.

Most of us are not as sophisticated about knowability and recognition as public figures and their agents might be. But we are nevertheless concerned about how many people know us and how well they know us. Our opinions about the extent of this knowability will vary from person to person. Some of us may find ourselves anxious to pursue intensely private styles of life, hoping for various reasons that few if any will know much about us at all. Then there are others who appear to be in constant pursuit of attention, doing anything necessary to gain it. Somewhere in the middle of these two dangerous extremes most of us will find ourselves.

We should indeed be concerned about how knowable we are, but not just for the profit motive. It is normal and right to want to be known and appreciated by a certain number of people within our circles of family and friends. We generally appreciate having those about us who will react to us, affirming us when we've done well, warning or chiding us if they see us headed toward error, and sharing with us in our sorrow or good fortune. We want to know that there are those who have looked deep inside us and appreciate or value what they've found.

Of course we will want the right to determine how far within us each of these will be able to look. Probably everyone has had the painful experience of being transparent with a person and then having that information used against us. It doesn't take too many bad experiences to make us cautious.

It is not unusual when one person in a relationship is open and the other more closed (or relatively untransparent) that the vulnerable party may be transparent for his friend—telling on him, putting words in his mouth, or sharing secrets that the other never meant to be disclosed. Trouble! The one who expresses himself easily needs to realize that this is a gross error in judgment, and it will create further isolation on the part of the quiet one. We cannot be transparent for another.

Relationships suffer serious damage, however, when one person chooses to avoid transparency at a level that is necessary to make that relationship work properly. More than once someone in a marriage has come to talk with us and related that the other spouse has rejected reasonable transparency, blocking off large parts of his or her life. A visitor says, "I don't know what he does with his money; where he spends large chunks of his time. I don't know what he thinks about me, about his job, about anything. We just don't know each other as well as I once thought we did."

To be sure, there is more than one reason this sort of withdrawal may have happened. Although it may be the action of the one who has retreated into unknowability, it is also possible that the one who complains has previously mistreated the privilege of sharing transparency, and that can be equally damaging to a relationship. We have to be careful to sense when that may have happened.

All of us know people who successfully shade the windows that lead into their lives. They do it by being extraordinarily silent or, when conversant, making sure that conversation is always centered on anything but themselves, refusing to ever express feelings, hopes, dreams, or struggles. Sometimes they cover themselves by keeping others at arm's length through the use of sarcasm, constant humor, or anger.

It is not a simple thing to open our lives to others. Yet until we do we will never be ready for any relationship of high value. Unwilling to be knowable, we will probably never enjoy a close friendship; it is possible that we will be frightened from making a marital commitment; and most likely we will never experience the joy of a team effort where a group accomplishes something together. So this matter of transparency is an important one. It should not be avoided, even though it is painful for some to research for themselves.

At the highest level of relationships—that of a person with his/her God—we will never enjoy a reach-and-touch experience until we have resolved the issue of transparency. No one who resists transparency will know Him.

The very first indication that there was something wrong in the relationship between Adam and God came when there was suddenly an absence of transparency on Adam's part. The Bible says that God came into the garden seeking Adam. But Adam hid. He was ashamed, he said, and apparently he didn't want anyone, especially God, to take note of his new-found condition of shame and embarrassment. There's no indication that he really understood what it was that was bothering him, but he seems to have known instinctively that whatever it was he didn't want the penetrating eyes of God to get hold of it. Thus, he hid, shutting the windows into his life for the first time.

He did the same thing with Eve. Trying to take the attention off himself, he attempted to put the blame for their problems on her. In fact he tried to place the accountability squarely upon the shoulders of Eve *and* God since, as he put it, He had placed Eve in the garden in the first place.

So both in his marriage to Eve and his walk with God, Adam became progressively unknowable. We can hardly appreciate the sadness of this fact unless we ponder the delights that must have been part of life before that moment, when the man and woman had been so close and intimate with one another that it could be said they were one flesh.

Perhaps it ought also be noted that Adam probably ceased being totally transparent with himself. In that he blamed Eve for his problems, he was lying not only to God but to himself. And when a person becomes wrapped in self-deceit, it is nothing more or less than a loss of transparency in the inward life.

Friendships can no more tolerate this sort of "unknowability" than one's relationship to God, to a spouse, or to self can. Of course there are friendships of varying levels and intensities, and the amount of transparency will always differ. But one thing is certain in all of these relationships: the amount of transparency must be reasonably mutual on both sides, or the friendship suffers.

Only in those relationships where there is an understood leader such as parent to child or mentor to disciple will the amount of transparency be different. An older Christian will not necessarily share every detail of life with the younger disciple, nor will a parent fully open his life to small children. That is neither practical nor wise. Here there will be selective transparency, with the wiser or older determining what is profitable for the other.

There can be destructiveness in relationships when we resist proper transparency. In the Peanuts cartoons, for example, there was once a moment when Lucy told Linus that she felt unusually crabby. But she didn't tell enough of the truth so that Linus could appreciate the full situation. And that's where her lack of transparency caused damage. Based on what he did know, Linus innocently suggested he might be of help. Bringing her a sandwich, cookies, and milk, he wanted to know if there was anything he had not thought of.

Now Lucy was forced to more transparency. "Yes," she said,

"there's one thing. . . . I DON'T WANT TO FEEL BETTER!"

Linus had a perfect right to frustration, even anger. He had performed in the relationship on the basis that there was reasonable transparency, but there wasn't. He'd taken time to reach out, but he was unable to touch because Lucy wasn't adequately knowable *or* touchable. She'd remained opaque, and as a result both she and Linus suffered.

You could say that Jesus Christ was a model of the transparent person. He was knowable to all who were interested, regardless of their economic status, sex, or spiritual condition. When someone asked where He lived, He said, "Come and see." When someone came to visit in the middle of the night, He was available. And when friends sought to entertain Him in their home, He was ready to accept.

He made his feelings known to those about Him when He knew they could handle them. At the grave of Lazarus He wept; with unjust and prejudiced men at the Temple He expressed anger. On another day He rejoiced, and on still another He revealed enormous sadness over the rigidity of some of His critics.

Jesus was willing to tell His personal objectives when questioned. He was responsive to those who came to Him seeking insight and wholeness. One of the most poignant pictures of His transparency comes when a woman came to anoint His head with expensive perfume (Mark 14:2-9). While others were critical and scolded her, He protected her. She alone had looked into His life and seen the suffering that was about to overcome Him. He permitted her to minister to Him in the days just before His anguish on the cross.

The Son of God would never have left behind the kind of men He did if He'd not opened His life to them. They were not theologians as such; they were students of life and stewardship, learning by walking and living with Him. They grew because His life was like Plato's intended home—one with a window into every room.

As we've said, transparency is a simple matter for some. It is not unusual for others of us to come into relationships desperately hoping that there are certain rooms in our lives we can keep shaded from view. In fact we may even board them up, terribly frightened that anyone will begin exploring in those areas of ourselves.

GORDON: A young man recently came to visit with me at my office. Since we'd not talked before, he filled the initial fifteen minutes of our interview with a personal introduction of himself. The first thing he wanted me to know was that he was a graduate of an Ivy League university. I actually got the impression that he waited for me to suck in my breathe with awe. Then he went on to inform me that he had an exceptional mind and that it was only a matter of time before the world awoke to his potential and made him a multimillionaire.

From there he moved on to his "connections," people he knew who were wealthy and powerful. Among his friends he numbered the presidents and CEO's of many major corporations. Finally, he shared with me some important theories he was developing about the performance of the stock market and how they would most likely revolutionize the financial world.

Following this rather remarkable introduction, I began to ask questions. You could say I was playing the Peeping Tom, looking through other windows of his life that he hadn't bothered to tell me about. And what answers! Because I poked, prodded, and pushed, I began to discover that underneath the cover-up was a man who was unhappy, disillusioned, failing at his job, struggling with his marriage, and concerned that his performance would never match his potential.

If I'd not searched out the closed windows, I would never have been able to help this young man. Our relationship would never have got off the ground. He was incapable of transparency at the start. There was too much fear of being found out.

What do people try to cover up when they fear transparency? The past, for one thing. For some of us there are hurts out of the preceding years caused by cruel or insensitive parents or friends. There have been humiliations or failures that have scarred our souls. Sometimes there are sins that we have committed and have never resolved. Out of this has flowed a river of guilt, and one can become paranoiac that if the windows are opened, everyone will find out.

A woman reveals that it is almost impossible for her to appreciate sexual intimacy with her husband. When he reaches out to touch her, her first instinct is to withdraw, to feel revulsion rather than love. When she fails to respond to him, he begins to feel that he has failed to be a loving man, and the relationship begins to hurt because he doubts himself and his capacity to make her happy.

But what is so tragic about this relationship is that it is the woman who, because of her inability to be transparent, is the cause of the hurt. For her struggle is not his fault; rather, at an early age—before their marriage—she had had previous sexual experience. And now in moments of intimacy she is constantly reminded of those times. Unable to deal with it before God, herself, or her husband, the guilt remains within and does a damaging work. Until she can open up the window of this room in her life with some responsible person and find forgiveness and healing, her marriage relationship will bear the stress of unknowability.

Other cover-ups that make us unknowable? We may seek to cover habits we cannot overcome. Or senses of inferiority: we feel ignorant, culturally substandard, unable to measure up to what we think are people's expectations.

We may imagine that few people would find us interesting or attractive should they ever come to know the "real us." We become convinced that self-exposure would draw ridicule, ostracism, or gossip. And all of that is liable to be reinforced if at any time we fall into a position of extreme vulnerability in which some unthinking or insensitive person does expose our inadequacy and bring upon us a painful consequence.

Most of us can remember more than one painful moment in our younger lives when friends cruelly revealed a secret about us that became the target of the peer group's laughter. Just a few humiliating experiences of that sort will guarantee increased secrecy, creating a possible pattern of introversion that could last a lifetime.

It is one thing to avoid transparency when with others. It is an even more serious matter when we slowly become less transparent to ourselves. As we noted before, this can be called self-deceit. Unable to face some truth about a part of our lives, we begin to suppress it, shading or bricking it over so that we don't have to keep facing the pain. The covering over can be done by lying to ourselves, blaming the event upon someone else, remaking the actual history into a story that is more suitable to our pride. Before long we have created a form of personal propaganda, which we not only share with others but come to believe ourselves.

GORDON: One of the families in our congregation, who have recently adopted a foster child, told me how the boy had faced up to the news that he would not be promoted out of kindergarten into first grade. "I decided," he told his new adoptive parents, "that if I stayed back I could help the teacher, and she really needs the help." At the age of six he has already mastered an adult game: rewriting history to cover up the pain of failure or shame.

Gail sometimes tells an audience of a night in our home when she entered the darkened bathroom and stumbled over a pair of shoes. Her first thought was, *Haven't I told this family often enough* not *to leave their shoes in the bathroom?* But having turned on the light to find out who was to blame, she discovered the shoes to be her own. She laughed out loud. But before the evidence was clear as to whose fault it was, she had protected herself by assuming that the problem was someone else's fault.

How can we become transparent people? Elizabeth O'Connor writes:

> I heard a story . . . which stays with me and continues to instruct. The central figure was an educated and cultured gentleman. One evening he stayed with two colleagues at his laboratory to work on a project they were all anxious to complete. When they had finished late that night, he invited them to his home for coffee. The conversation moved from their work at the lab to art, and he fell to sharing with them his interest in Greek architecture. Remembering a new volume that he had on the subject, he took it down from the shelf and handed it to his more advantaged co-worker, who quickly glanced at the pages and returned it to him. He was already putting the book back on the shelf when he glimpsed from the corner of his eye the hand of the other man extended to receive the book. The picture hardly registered. He did not come to terms with what had happened until he was in bed. And then he saw again the hand of the other man reaching to receive the book he had never offered. All unconsciously he had made the judgment that this man, being self-tutored, would not be interested in art. In an automatic way, he had excluded him.
>
> The scientist had not thought himself capable of treating another fellow human like this, but *he had enough understanding to know that this was not an isolated incident in his life. It was a glimpse of something in himself of which he was only dimly aware.* He left his bed, and spent the rest of the night sitting in his study reflecting on what had happened. *He wanted the picture of it burned in his mind and heart* so that it would keep him alert and help him avoid the possibility of his going through life ignoring the outstretched hands of his friends.[1] (Italics added)

In terms of transparency, we will never be able to engage in healthy relationships until we have labored to know ourselves. And when we have achieved a healthy ruthlessness with ourselves, then various windows may begin to open up. What fears, what shames, what disappointments, what guilts, and what humiliations mark the

---

1. Elizabeth O'Connor, *Search for Silence* (Waco, Tex.: Word, 1972), pp. 40-41.

back rooms of our lives? Have they been shaded over? Even to ourselves? Whether we know it or not, they will make us much less knowable to others until they are dealt with one by one and resolved in God's forgiveness and our acceptance.

That sort of transparency paves the way to the most important of our relationships: the one we have with God. Isaiah, the great prophet of Israel, began his public ministry with a vision of God in the Temple. The very first thing that came to him in those extraordinary moments when he was in God's presence was a sudden experience of self-knowledge. And the new awareness was painful, for it was not an attractive view. But still, before he could be of any use to anyone else, that knowledge of himself, which he had apparently covered up, had to be established and renewed every day.

C. S. Lewis wrote of this ruthless self-knowledge to an American friend when she was tempted to become preoccupied with another person's faults. "Try not to think—much less, speak—of their sins. One's own are a much more profitable theme! And if, on consideration, *one can find no faults on one's own side, then cry for mercy: for this must be a most dangerous delusion*" (Italics added).[2]

In spiritual language, transparency can sometimes be called brokenness. It is not unusual to see in the Bible great and godly men and women who came before God transparent and broken. Nehemiah is one of those. Brooding upon the ruins of Jerusalem and seeking a reason for God's lifting His protective hand from the city, Nehemiah concluded, "I and my father's house have sinned. We have acted very corruptly" (Nehemiah 1:6-7, RSV).

When a person becomes capable of this self knowledge and is rightly broken before God, that is the first and perhaps most important step to learning how to be transparent with others.

GAIL: In the early days of our marriage, both of us had to deal with this issue of transparency. For example, in our occasional conflicts it was difficult for me to confess the possibility of being wrong. Why? Because, strange as it may seem, there was an imbedded fear that if Gordon ever found out that I had imperfections in my life, he might abandon me. He'd never communicated that, but somehow I'd carried that sort of reaction into

---

2. C. S. Lewis, *Letters to an American Lady*, ed. Clyde S. Kilby (Grand Rapids: Eerdmans, 1967, published in conjunction with Pyramid Publications, 1975), p. 95.

our marriage. Now many years later, it may seem silly to actually have ever thought that one partner in a marriage would desert the other over a simple little revelation of an imperfection. Of course, Gordon would not have ever left, but I nevertheless felt real fear. So transparency came hard for me; I was worried over its possible consequences. I was living with this hidden fear that made it difficult for me to be transparent enough with Gordon to say, "I'm sorry; I was really wrong on that issue."

GORDON: With a few years of assurance between ourselves, that fear was slowly dissolved. But now I know that Gail had a real fear, and it had to be confronted and treated. Not to have faced it would have meant that in our relationship there would have been a significant area closed to the view of the other person. It would have hurt us badly in the long run if it had not been carefully treated.

GAIL: Gordon had to realize why there was this tendency on my part toward cover-up and resistance to repentance. What he had to do was to repeatedly assure me that he loved me unconditionally. In effect he had to remind me, "It's all right to be wrong on occasion. I love you anyway; I won't leave you."

GORDON: Perhaps it's worth adding that if I'd wanted to, I could have taken advantage of Gail's concern and used it against her whenever I wanted to manipulate the relationship for my own ends. I'm reminded of that whenever I hear a frustrated mother in a large store say to her reluctant preschooler, "If you don't behave, I'm going to walk off and leave you here by yourself." In a relationship you care about, you don't do things like that. No, the key was to encourage Gail's transparency, and as she achieved it, both of us grew as a result.

So important has this learning experience been that we realized it was a key lesson in the character development of our children. If we expected them to be transparent with us and later on with others, we had to demonstrate transparency for them first of all in our lives. It meant admitting when we didn't know answers, when we were wrong and needed to apologize, when we were a bit scared of something, and when we knew that there were certain realities in our lives that were bigger than all of us. Our children had to see us as real people; the windows had to be opened.

> GAIL: We learned that from Gordon. He has always been the instigator of what he has called in the pulpit "the repentant life-style." I have come to strongly believe as I view our lives with the children that this life-style, more than anything else, has made their pastor-dad a genuine co-struggler in the Christian life. It was, in fact, what made it possible for them to admit defeat or failure because he taught us all by example to admit that we are far from perfect. In talking to many women who have never heard their proud husbands admit fault, eventually they and their children see discrepancy between what is and what is claimed and lose respect.
>
> GORDON: Remember when Billy Graham's small grandson fell while he was running to his mother? He quickly got up, brushed himself off, and said, "Oops, I dropped myself!" How's that for not taking yourself too seriously? Well, we have tried to see imperfection in our home in much the same way. It's to be expected. As leader in our home, I am no exception but must be first performer in facing that fact.

When we are not transparent with one another in our relationships, people fall victim to an unrealistic, unwholesome view of true humanity. Because the windows are shaded over, we begin to treat each other on the basis of serious distortions. Take, for example, the words of a woman who once wrote to Bruce Larson:

> My husband is a much-beloved church leader, praised and admired. Doctors tell me he is psychotic, a very sick man. When you see the one you love so much turning bitterly hostile, drawing further and further away in a shell of loneliness, yet still teaching all the truth, there is a continuing grief that cannot be expressed.
>
> Every attempt at help is blocked. Every expression of love is interpreted in the wrong way. *And all the while his Christian friends admire and praise him and force him further and further into his prison of loneliness, where any admission of fault or failure becomes so threatening that it seems to mean destruction.*[3] (Italics added)

3. Bruce Larson, *No Longer Strangers* (Waco, Tex.: Word, 1976).

Here is one more case of a person let down in relationships. Failures and weaknesses are compounded because, first of all, a man has elected to cover up enough of himself that people wrongly assume that he is a fully functioning Christian. So they are a victim of his unknowability. But they are at fault in that church for their false understanding.

Thus it becomes increasingly clear that if we wish to enjoy healthy relationships in our friendships, our families, or our marriages, this question of transparency must be examined and managed. How much of ourselves are we willing to reveal to others?

Opening the windows to ourselves is risky business. When we disclose our personal lives to others in a relationship, we will always face the possibility that what we have placed in their hands may be mishandled. Our confidence could be betrayed. There could be misinterpretations of our words and feelings. Yes, the risk is that one might even turn against us. Sooner or later something unfortunate could indeed happen.

Naturally, a wise person does not open his life to everyone. And one makes sure that the other party is ready to handle whatever it is that is disclosed. Jesus, John writes in chapter 2 of his gospel, did not trust Himself to the Jerusalem crowd, "For he knew their hearts." Knowing their priorities and their motives, Jesus withdrew rather than become totally transparent at that moment.

But although there may be cause for some caution, the overly cautious, who resist any form of transparency, taste a loneliness and solitude that is devastating to the soul.

When a person in a friendship or a marriage relationship determines to pursue transparency, what are some of the areas that begin to become unshaded?

It is likely that conversation will begin to take on a three-dimensional nature: experiences from the past, thoughts in the present, and expectations of the future.

From the past will come an increasing stream of memories of formative experiences: joys and delights, sorrows and hurts. To the surface comes a record of striking moments when there were great learning experiences and penetrating failures. We begin to appreciate the richness of what formed another out of the past, and we become the more sensitive and caring because we have been allowed to see down the corridors of one's innermost being.

In the present, we will begin to learn about one's feelings, convictons, and concerns, one's sense of determinaton about issues and possibilities.

And in the futurist sense, we begin to hear of dreams and fantasies. And in such transparency, two marital partners or several friends begin to plot the course of their lives together, making sure that the tracks move closer together rather than farther apart.

In a relationship where there is transparency there can be enormous growth. For as the windows become unshaded, we permit others to offer light to our opinions, our concerns, and our dreams. They help complete our thoughts, balance our extremes, and correct our miscalculations. We are reminded of parallel situations that we may have forgotten and that now bring encouragement, direction, or prevention. They may have shared with us the very keys of life, which may escalate our maturity or protect us from destruction. But transparency has to happen first.

When the architect first came to Plato with his offer to build a very private house, he thought he had a special thing to offer. But Plato saw it all differently. A healthy life in a home is a transparent one, he believed. And that demands more windows than walls. What Plato knew about homes, we must learn about relationships. The question is: Are we building walls or opening windows?

4

I Can See Right Through You

In one of his books Leonard Griffith has recalled the story of a physician, Dr. Roger Pilkington, who once journeyed to South Wales to give a series of lectures. Arriving at his hotel much later than he'd expected, he was told by a "tired looking and pale middle-aged receptionist" that only a cold supper would be available. "But if you come into the office any time after nine o'clock you can have a cup of tea," she said.

Later in the evening after his lecture, Pilkington returned to the hotel and decided to accept the offer of a cup of tea. When he went to the office he found the receptionist conversing with other guests on the subject of suicide. Assuming that he was a medical doctor, she began to ask him a series of questions about methods of suicide and the possibilities of pain associated with each form. Later, Pilkington, having finished his tea, went to his room.

But, Griffith says, the doctor could not sleep. "He had been lying wide-awake for a few minutes when a feeling came over him which he describes as 'a sense of being charged like a condenser.' Throwing on his dressing gown, he ran down four flights of stairs, walked straight into the inner office, confronted the receptionist and asked bluntly, 'I want to know why you are going to commit suicide.' She began to protest, but Dr. Pilkington cut her short. 'I know you're going to. I shall not stop you. But you must tell me why you are going to do it.' "

The woman began to tell the doctor her story. Her father had suffered from a disease that caused blindness, and now her physician had informed her that the disease was hereditary and that she would have to prepare herself for the same result. She was contemplating suicide rather than face the awful consequences she had seen her father experience.

Pilkington, a specialist in genetics, asked a number of questions of the receptionist, and when he had assembled the data he concluded that the disease was not, in fact, hereditary. And he convinced her of his findings. It was a freeing moment for this woman who had come close to terminating her life. "You can go back to bed. I know you are not deceiving me," she told him. "Don't worry. I shall not kill myself tonight or ever."[1]

What was it that drove a tired man from his bed that night and compelled him to confront the receptionist in such a way that he was able to save her life? We call it *sensitivity.*

What is it? Sensitivity is the unique capacity to see, hear, or feel the realities beneath the surface and to discern the appropriate action or response. Pilkington, for example, had been in a room with several others engaged in a conversation. But he was the only one of the group who heard something beneath the surface that ultimately propelled him into motion.

Others had heard the same words; others had enjoyed the same pleasant, if not morbid, exchange of information. But only one person finally sensed that there was a deeper agenda hidden beneath the words of the hotel receptionist. He alone seemed able to conclude that another human being needed help. To hear what he heard and do what he did about it is sensitivity.

Our starting point was the command of Jesus Christ to the disciples concerning their love for one another. It was a love, He said, that should be modeled after His love for them. And when the life of Christ is analyzed, it will clearly demonstrate that Jesus was a master of sensitivity. His capacity to look into things and discern true need as well as true evil was remarkable.

No one profited more from Jesus' sensitivity than Peter. Think of one of the earliest recorded encounters between the two when Peter fell on his knees before Christ. Peter hardly understood himself. You could say that he was intimidated by what he perceived to be the awesome power and capacity of Jesus. "Go away from me, Lord; I am a sinful man!" he managed to babble (Luke 5:8). But the sensitive Christ knew better than to trust surface words. He knew fear in a

---

1. Leonard Griffith, *God in Man's Experience* (Waco, Tex.: Word, 1968), pp. 121-22.

man when He saw it, and He was able to set the fisherman at ease. "Peter, don't be afraid," the Lord told him. It was the beginning of an incredible friendship.

Later in the training process when Peter made another dramatic gesture, this time to step forward affirming that Jesus was in fact the Christ, the Lord was sensitive enough to know that Peter needed to be recognized and encouraged for his step of faith. But when Peter almost immediately protested against Jesus' revelation of His own coming death, Christ was just as sensitive again to know that the fisherman now needed a strong rebuke.

It was Jesus who was insightful enough to know when the disciples were confused about the nature of greatness and penetrated their silence to raise their questions to the surface. He was discerning about the protests the twelve made of their faithfulness, knowing that they could not keep their promises. Rather than accept their intended loyalty, He made quite plain, especially to Peter, that He fully understood their weakness and was already praying for them in the hour of their trial.

Each time you take a look, Jesus seems to have been one step ahead of everyone else, because He saw what virtually no one else saw. Why? Because Jesus was the most sensitive person who ever lived.

Again, what is sensitivity? On a physiological level, it is the ability to make judgments about something through touch or taste or sight or sound or smell. Those areas are sometimes called the five senses, and when they are fully operative, they make enormous amounts of information available to a person upon which he can act.

We once spent a day in an up-country West African village, where people who suffered from Hanson's disease (once known as leprosy) lived. While there we learned that the reason people with this disease often lose fingers, toes, or other extremities is they are no longer able to sense pain due to insensitive nerve endings. Unable to perceive heat, they are liable to burn their fingers over a fire. Not feeling the bite of a spider, they are ignorant of the fact that poison has been injected into their systems. Unaware that they have cut themselves, they do not know of the possibility of infection. Physiologically, they are not sensitive people.

If people enter into marriage or friendship with their relational nerve endings inoperative because they are damaged or because they have never been developed, then there are going to be lots of problems—hurts, misunderstandings, conflicts. Someone is going to have to give in a lot more than should be necessary because the insensitive person is simply not going to be aware of what is going on inside the people in his world.

You can see this issue arising as early as the garden in which Adam and Eve lived. When Adam sinned and lost his transparency, the effect was immediate and tragic. Eve, his wife, could no longer enjoy that natural intimacy of fully knowing him. The Scriptures had called it being "one flesh." There were shades, so to speak, over Adam's windows. Now the challenge to "decode" Adam began. How could she really know what was going on within her husband? What was he thinking, feeling, struggling with, wondering about? How could she know?

> GORDON: Occasionally, Gail will look into my eyes and discern exactly what I'm thinking. I couldn't lie to her if I tried, and I can hardly keep a secret. "I can see right through you," she says. And I suspect she can.
>
> But not as well as Eve could see through Adam before sin destroyed the transparency. Then there were no secrets, because there were no shames. At best Gail can approximate what she thinks she sees in me. But I must admit she does well at it.

How could Eve figure out Adam? For one thing, Eve would now have to depend to a considerable extent upon what Adam told her about himself if she were to understand and appreciate the deeper, now hidden, dimensions of her husband. She'd have to listen to and weigh his words. She would have to watch his face and body language. And as she worked at it, she'd learn to pay as much attention to what he didn't say or do.

But even then there would be a limit to the extent to which she could look within Adam and determine what he was really like. He would have to work at transparency if she was to know him well; and she would have to work at the counterpart of transparency, her sensitivity to what he was as a person. The two go together to make a relationship healthy. One demands the presence of the other.

But many people are not sensitive people from a relational point of view. They do not take the time to acquire the ability to find out what is going on within another person. They are not aware when others feel intimidated, when they are hurting, when they are sad or happy, or when they wish to be heard. To the extent that one partner in a friendship or a marriage, for example, is not sensitive, that relationship will be frankly impaired.

It is no secret that, for the most part, women tend to be more sensitive than men. The reason for this has often been debated. But the fact that women are far more intuitive has been demonstrated in many different research projects.

In her best-selling book *Unfinished Business,* Maggie Scarf notes a recent study done at Yale University on the subject of depression among college students. "When females were depressed," writes Scarf, "they suffered 'significantly higher levels of . . . experiences of loneliness, helplessness, dependency and the need for external sources of security.' But for males in contrast, depression had to do much more with 'self criticism and the failure to live up to expectation.' "[2]

Women, Maggie Scarf concluded, become depressed about the insufficiency of relationships, whereas men tend to become depressed about their failure to achieve, to "make it, to gain control of and mastery over the environment."[3]

The significance of that study is found in the importance women place on relationships. Because they are much more concerned about the health of relationships in which they are involved, *they are liable to be more sensitive as to what makes the relationships work and what issues and atmospheres are causing the relationship to falter.*

Many men, on the other hand, may tend to ignore the priority of their relationships because they have a stronger desire to achieve and accumulate things. And they are negligent in determining what may be wrong until it is almost too late to do anything about it. Only when trouble is obvious and unavoidable are many men willing to act.

We have had scores of experiences in which a wife has come seeking help for a deteriorating marriage. The husband shows little or no inclination to seek assistance until, as we sometimes put it, the roof falls in. Rightly or wrongly, in desperation the wife may have decided to leave the home. Then the husband may suddenly come to attention. He realizes the seriousness of what he has been doing or not doing. He comes rushing to the counselor or pastor ready to make any change, go to any extreme to get his wife back. Unfortunately, he is often too late. What happened? He didn't develop his sensitivities to the relationship. He didn't see or hear what was really going on. In short, he never really took time to know his wife.

Just being female does not make a person sensitive. We know many women who are extremely insensitive to what is going on in

2. Maggi Scarf, *Unfinished Business: Pressure Points in the Lives of Women* (New York: Ballantine, 1980), p. 96.
3. Ibid.

the lives of people around them. The fact is that they may be too concerned about themselves to spend time monitoring the affairs of anyone else.

We are thinking of a family, for example, where a widow and widower have decided to marry. The daughter of the widower has refused to give her blessing (as if it were asked) to the marriage because all she can think about is the intrusion the new wife will be upon her relationship with her father. She will lose her special intimacy with him; she will probably have to move out of his home; she will have to face the fact that another woman is going to influence her father. And because the marriage threatens her, she is against it. It does not occur to her that her father is terribly lonely and has found someone with whom he can share marital love. She has not taken the time to sense his needs because she is too concerned about her own.

A woman may not develop sensitivity to others in her world because her natural beauty has made her the center of attention for so long that she has never learned to reach out to anyone else. A man may never develop sensitivity because he has assets in terms of money, or charisma, or physical size that make everyone quickly accept his way of doing things. He doesn't need to understand others because they will have to understand him, or else. Thus, he is never aware when he says or does things that terribly wound spouse or friends. Such people do not know when their moods have injured others, and they do not know when their decisions or actions have seriously inconvenienced the lives of those about them.

GORDON: When our teenage children were babies, we used to laugh about something called the "mother's ear." It was supposed to function during the night. As long as Gail was nursing our tiny ones, her mother's ear was extremely sensitive. It could pick up the slightest stir in the cradle. But for some unexplainable reason, when nursing days were over, the mother's ear seemed to transfer to me. Suddenly I was the one who could hear the slightest sound coming from the bed of the growing children. I never quite understood how that transfer took place, and Gail wasn't prepared to enlighten me.

But our Lord was never like that, even when He was under enormous pressure. It is worth noting His sensitivities while on the cross. He was concerned, for example, about forgiveness for His enemies; "Father, forgive them. . . ." He was responsive to the cry of hope from the thief who was off to one side: "Today you will be with me." And then, in a most beautiful and tender moment, He expressed His strong concern for the welfare of His mother. He had to make sure that John would take care of her: "Here is your mother." All of that while He agonized through His own coming death. That is sensitivity.

Sensitivity means an ear of sorts is working. It hears not only words but the tone in which the words are spoken. It takes note of words not spoken, of silences, of unuttered groans and sighs. Sensitivity means an eye that sees fatigue, unhappiness, expectancy, loneliness, or hurt. Sensitivity means a touch that discerns tension or weakness, energy or relaxation.

E. Stanley Jones writes:

> You can judge how far you have risen in the scale of life by asking one question: How wisely and how deeply do I care? . . . To be Christianized is to be sensitized: Christians are people who care. No one, anywhere, can come into authentic contact with Jesus Christ in personal surrender and obedience without beginning to care. It was the first reaction I felt when I arose from my knees in the hour of conversion. I felt as though I wanted to put my arms around the world and share this with everybody.[4]

> GORDON: When we were first married, I quickly discovered that Gail had an extraordinary gift of sensitivity. It came out in various ways. For example, on the way home from a party or a Bible study, Gail might refer to a conversation I'd been carrying on and say, "Didn't you hear what he was really trying to tell you? He was upset that he'd been overlooked and forgotten in that discussion. You didn't pick that up at all, did you?"
>
> No, the fact was that I hadn't. Frankly, sometimes it irritated me that Gail would claim to pick up signals that I hadn't seen or heard at all. But over and over again when I would take time the next day to check into Gail's observations, I would discover that she had correctly discerned the situation. I was listening to words; but Gail was listening to something deeper and far more significant.

4. E. Stanley Jones, *A Song of Ascents* (Nashville: Abingdon, 1979), p. 291.

I knew that if I was ever going to be a leader of people, I'd have to acquire the sensitivity that Gail handled so well. And I was years behind her in that department. She'd been developing her sensitivity throughout her teen years, long before we'd met. She made sensitivity a matter of prayer, asking God to help her to see things in people that others were not looking hard enough to see. In those same days, I was struggling just to understand myself. No wonder she was the more sensitive.

GAIL: But Gordon tried hard to make up for lost time. He learned to ask me a lot of questions about the things I was seeing and hearing. And most important, he didn't react negatively when I pointed out something he'd missed. Little by little he learned how to read the hidden messages in people: a facial expression, a word said in a certain way, body language, a sigh. He began to see into situations in groups: who was the hostile one, who was the intimidated one. He learned how to bring people together by figuring out what each needed from the other in order for there to be peace. He worked at it, and he's proof that sensitivity can be learned.

Can sensitivity really be acquired? Yes, if one determines that he will work hard to attain it. One must believe that God meant for every one of us to be able to reach out and touch another through sensitivity.

We believe that it is God's will that everyone pursue sensitivity, for it is the gateway to the kind of caring necessary in the marriage, the family, among friends, and in the congregation.

GAIL: When I think of sensitivity, my mind often turns to a woman we met in Hawaii. Ruth was an impressive person because she often used her sensitivity to reach people who came to visit her church. We learned about Ruth's sensitivity from a businessman whose name was Ike, now a leader in Ruth's congregation.

When Gordon asked him how he had come to faith in Christ, Ike shared with us how he had grown up a Buddhist. But his children were drawn to life at a local Protestant church, and Ike would drive them to Sunday school each week. Sometimes he would go off and leave them at the front door and return at the end of the morning. But it was not unusual for him to sit on the front steps of the church for a long while, waiting for the conclusion of Sunday school.

It was Ruth who took note of this routine, Ike told us. And one day when he was sitting by himself she walked up and presented him with a beautiful orchid lei that she had made. It was just the thing to make a lonely man feel accepted, and it drew him into the building where he heard the gospel preached and later chose to follow Christ. Ike was won by Ruth's sensitivity and caring.

One wonders how many people could be touched, how many relationships healed, if many of us were to set out to acquire sensitivity. And if we did, where would we begin?

1. *Pray for it.* Sensitivity is in part a gift of God's Spirit. No more beautiful picture of sensitivity is seen in the Bible than that of the shepherd who cares for the sheep. He knows when they need the coolness and refreshment of green pastures and quiet streams. He is aware when the flock requires a "table" set in the presence of feared enemies. Shepherds sense when there is the necessity for guidance through a dark valley or when it is time to go out to seek a lost lamb. They understand the vulnerability of the sheep and therefore stand at the door of the sheepfold, turning away predators.

It is those qualities that Jesus willed to His people. But they are gained by prayer, by reflection and meditation, by careful and consistent practice.

2. *Study sensitivity in the Bible,* in the lives of great saints, and in the performance of mature people about you. Among the most sensitive people in the Bible are David, John, and Mary, the mother of the Lord. Timothy was a sensitive person; so was Luke.

We learn sensitivity by watching mature men and women who are remarkably perceptive in groups, in marriages and families, in friendships. If we develop a curiosity about the way they respond to situations, the things they listen and look for, the conclusions to which they come when they are dealing with people, we will learn fast. It's important to ask sensitive people questions about how they have come to discern things the way that they do.

A close friend of ours is a physician. Once he told us how important he found calling upon a patient just before he or she went into surgery. He was aware that all surgical patients (especially first-timers) have tremendous anxieties. Will something go wrong? Will they come out of the anesthetic? He had come to realize the importance of speaking to those fears by giving a word of hope.

"I always make sure that I review the surgical procedure with them, and then I conclude by saying to them, 'And when you are in the recovery room and begin to wake up, I will come in and see you and tell you how everything went.'" That assurance that he would be coming to see them usually rested the worst of fears. It was a word of hope, and it brought peace to troubled minds. That is sensitivity.

3. Another friend suggests that those seeking to become sensitive in relationships *"watch the streets."* She got the idea, she said, from Solomon, who observed that there are objects lessons everywhere that will teach us about how people feel and what they need.

One day our friend Barbara was waiting her turn in a long checkout line at Sears. Some of the customers were hostile and aggressive. But the clerk at the cash register seemed to have everything under control.

When Barbara reached the clerk, she asked her how she could remain so calm in the midst of such abuse. "Well," said the woman, "I've got eight children. I learned a long time ago not to sweat the small stuff."

It was a short encounter, but Barbara, sensitive to the mature performance of a person under fire, had asked a question and got a pithy, insightful answer—one she immediately began to apply in her own life. And it was learned in the "streets." Sensitivity comes as we study others and what makes them as they are. We watch for superior performance and ask what it means as our friend Barbara did, and we note poor performance and speculate on what is behind it.

Questions go to the heart of things, and the answers help us to build up an information bank that helps us to understand people we meet.

When Jesus had talked with the disciples concerning His coming execution in Jerusalem, the Scripture says, "They did not understand the saying, and they were afraid to ask him." The failure of the twelve to look into things and ask questions when they had the chance is a key to their pathetic response to crises on the night of Jesus' betrayal. They hadn't been curious enough to learn.

Their failure to question also points up their insensitivity to Christ. If they had thought through what He was saying to them, that might have given them cause to care for Him far more intensely, to have been more of a friend to Him in His lonely and suffering hours. But they weren't sensitive enough to ask the right questions. Thus they remained on the surface of events and people when they should have been developing discernment.

4. Sensitivity is learned when we *"sit where they sit."* Those are

words from the early part of the book of Ezekiel, where God challenged Ezekiel to become aware of the needs of the people about him who were suffering. And when he went and sat where they sat for seven days, he was overwhelmed with the realities of their situation.

If we are going to be sensitive people, we will have to accept the fact that there will be difficult moments. Sensitive people share the sufferings of others. They take on feelings, pains, predicaments, and consequences. That is how sensitivity is learned.

GAIL: When I choose a core leader for our Grace Chapel Bible study, I look for a person who has tasted suffering. I want leaders who are not oblivious to the stresses and struggles of the women for whom they'll be responsible. A pastor's wife who heard me say that couldn't understand why that would make such a difference. Then she passed through a year of deep depression and discovered a whole new side to life, a painful side. She saw others in an entirely different light. Later she said to me, "Now I know why you look for people who've experienced pain. My core leader knows what depression is all about, and her experience with it has given her the heart to identify with me and not simply preach at me with surface platitudes and clichés."

When we too have hurt, we know something of what another person needs when he is lonely, or defeated, or feeling a failure. We are not glib with answers or advice.

GORDON: The other day we were talking with a friend who attends another church and has been struggling with cancer. I asked if his pastor was an encouragement to him, and I'll never forget his response. He said, "Frankly, Gordon, I kind of hate to see the pastor come around. He spends all of his time telling me how I *ought* to feel. He never asks how I actually feel and offers me a chance to express myself. I end up feeling guilty that I'm not quite living up to what he thinks I ought to be doing." It was a lesson to me. Christians can be so insensitive in the midst of all our good intentions. Here was a sad example of that sort of thing.

A loving couple in our congregation faced the divorce of one of their children. They were shocked at how few people could speak to them for several months about the situation. At first they felt reject- ed. But because of their maturity, they eventually realized that most people simply didn't know what to say; so they had said nothing. Later, they told us that people in relational pain do not need an- swers, only a touch, only a reminder that friends are praying, caring, and still love them. Only those who'd gone through similar exper- iences knew what to say to them. Again, it was those who'd sat where they sat.

5. We aggressively *open ears and eyes*. The agenda for the sensi- tive person: I will treat people the way they need to be treated, not the way they deserve to be treated.

"Hello! Is there anyone out there who will listen to me? How can I convince you that I am a prisoner? For the past five years I have not seen a park or the ocean or even just a few feet of grass." So writes an eighty-four-year-old woman from a nursing home, who has been neglected and ignored.

> Most of the nurse's aides who work here are from other countries. Even those who can speak English don't have much in common with us. So they hurry to get their work done as quickly as possible. There are a few caring people who work here, but there are so many of us who are needy for that kind of honest attention.
>
> A doctor comes to see me once a month. He spends approximately three to five seconds with me and then a few more minutes writing in the chart or joking with the nurses. . . . I sometimes wonder about how the nurses' aides feel when they work so hard for so little money and then see that the person who spends so little time is the one who is paid the most.

This is a person crying to be heard, and no one is listening. She is one of millions whose voice is not monitored.

> I am writing this because many of you may live to be old like me, and by then it will be too late. You, too, will be stuck here and wonder why nothing is being done, and you, too, will wonder if there is any justice in life. Right now I pray every night that I may die in my sleep and get this nightmare of what someone has called life over with, if it means living in this prison day after day.[5]

5. *Hartford Courant*, 5 October 1979, p. 25.

GAIL: One day a man stepped to the front of the sanctuary at Grace Chapel to say a word to Gordon. He recalled an earlier Sunday when, in response to Gordon's public invitation at the end of a service, he'd come forward, knelt, and received Christ as his Savior. He told my husband that what he remembered most about that day was that it was the first time in months that any one had physically touched him, looked him in the eye, and given him undivided attention for five minutes.

GORDON: I remember the day he came. He was a very sad looking person; he seemed so desperate. It was natural to just put an arm around him for a moment and then look him straight in the eye and talk about the things that were a struggle to him. I never realized how much it would mean to him. It's frightening, isn't it? How many others need that touch and that attentive ear and eye. And we're frequently missing them because we aren't sensitive to their need.

GAIL: But it's not just at church. It's in apartments and homes, where singles share living accommodations. In families, where we are becoming too busy to practice sensitivity toward one another. In the office, where life is being pursued at such a high pitch that it becomes impossible to hear if anyone is crying.

But when we open our ears and our eyes to watch and listen, we need to search not only for needs but also for people's weak spots. Some people need our protection. Others need us to know when to back off. And still others just don't need our right answers and our correct opinions at every moment.

Richard Foster in *Celebration of Discipline* tells of a debate that took place between the brilliant Quaker George Fox and an acquaintance, Nathaniel Stephens. Fox, with his incredible mind, quickly overwhelmed Stephens almost to the point of humiliation. And Stephens said, "Mr. Fox, I fear your sunlight has blocked out my starlight."[6]

Fox had to learn something about sensitivity on that occasion.

In healthy relationships we learn to ask the question What does this person need that I can give? A father learns when his son needs

6. Richard Foster, *The Celebration of Discipline* (San Francisco: Harper & Row, 1978), p. 162.

an encouraging word or a rebuke. He learns when his daughter needs affection and when she needs a male figure who will believe in her capabilities as a person. A woman learns when her husband needs to be left alone and when he needs her quiet presence. A mentor learns when the disciple needs a quick answer and when he needs to find it out for himself. In so doing we are expressing sensitivity.

Catherine Booth, co-founder of the Salvation Army, was a remarkably sensitive person. And her discernment showed best in her relationship to William, her husband. In a letter written to him, she declares her intent that their home will always be a place sensitive to his needs and concerns:

> I am delighted; it makes me happy to hear you speak as you do about home. Yes, if you will seek home, love home, be happy at home, I will spend my energies in trying to make it a more than ordinary one; it shall, if my ability can do it, be a spot sunny and bright, pure and calm, refined and tender, a fit school in which to train immortal spirits for a holy and glorious heaven; a fit resting-place for a spirit pressed and anxious about public duties; but Oh, I know it is easy to talk, I feel how liable I am to fall short; but it is well to purpose right, to aim high, to hope much; yes, we will make home to each other the brightest spot on earth, we will be tender, thoughtful, loving, and forbearing, will we not? Yes, we will.[7]

These are the words of a woman who was reaching out to touch, who had looked within a man and found something to which she could minister.

It was sensitivity that caused a man like Roger Pilkington to reach out and touch a lonely, frightened hotel receptionist who might otherwise have taken her life out of ignorance of her real situation. Sensitivity is a necessary element in any marriage, in any family, in any friendship, making it possible for us to love one another just as Christ loved His disciples.

---

7. Harold Begbie, *Life of General William Booth* (New York: Macmillan, 1920), p. 172.

5

The Many Levels of Talk, Part 1

Gustav Mahler was a brilliant musician and composer. But expertise in one area of life does not guarantee skill in another. Apparently, Mahler's capacities to relate to others left something to be desired. His life was marked with examples of how not to win friends and influence people.

Noted conductor Bruno Walter, who wrote Mahler's biography, tells of a hot June day when a hopeful young composer came to the maestro's studio, hoping to gain his acceptance of a newly written opera. Mr. Walter left the two alone to examine the score at the keyboard, and returned some time later.

> I joined them toward the end of the last scene and found them in their shirt-sleeves, the composer perspiring profusely and Mahler obviously sunk in the depths of boredom and aversion. When the playing had ended, Mahler did not utter a word. The composer, too, probably deeply hurt by Mahler's silence, said nothing, and I saw no chance of saving the awkward situation by any effort of my own. There was no help for it: the composer put on his coat, wrapped up his score, and after a silence that lasted for several minutes and a coldly polite "Auf wiedersehen" terminated the painful scene. An entire life time of personal relations of all kinds had not supplied Mahler with that modicum of social polish which would have brought the meeting to an ordinary end.[1]

1. Bruno Walter, *Themes and Variations; an Autobiography* trans. James Gulston (New York: Knopf, 1946), p. 51.

It would have seemed easy for a perceptive man to have saved the feelings of a young aspiring composer—if he knew the words to say and how to say them. But Mahler was not a communicator under such circumstances. As a result, a young man desperate for approval and encouragement from another whose judgment counted for something was left angry, empty, and humiliated.

To reach out and touch is to communicate, to cross invisible barriers with specific messages that bare the heart and mind of a human being and bring two or more people together. Perhaps the simplest and the most difficult thing for many people to do in friendship, family relationships or marriages is to talk—to talk in such a way that there is a satisfying exchange that leaves everyone in a state of fulfillment and wholeness.

How did Christ love His disciples? He communicated with them—in a score of ways. He told them stories; He answered endless questions; He gave directives about life; He opened up the mysteries of Scripture; He disclosed to them His expectations about the future.

On the other hand, He was a listener, responding to their anxieties and concerns. He watched them carefully and knew the intent of their hearts and minds at every moment. Jesus not only reached out; He was in touch in every possible way.

If there was doubt in a man's voice or actions, Jesus was gentle with the weakness but firm in bringing the doubter face to face with the truth. If others misjudged the motives of a well-meaning person, Jesus was quick to sort out the issues and remove the confusion. Wherever Christ was, there was sure to be maximum light on the moment because Jesus was a communicator; He made sure everyone was in full possession of the facts.

Many relationships suffer from a lack of communication. And where people cannot either speak their mind in a way conducive to the situation or comprehend what others are saying, there is apt to be trouble. Relationships with minimal communication are intolerable, even destructive.

A friend who is the president of a large company tells of a vice president in his firm who had to be dismissed. The reason? "He was a brilliant executive," our friend said, "but the fact was that he couldn't get along with anybody. You never really knew what he was thinking, and he wasn't about to tell you. He became a liability rather than an asset. He simply had to go."

Human beings communicate in a score of ways with one another. We can discern what another is thinking, for example, as we note what some call *body language:* what others are doing with their hands, the gestures they are making, or their posture (rigid or relaxed). We communicate with our faces: through frowns and smiles, the use of our eyes (seducing, laughing, sad). We communicate with our smells when we take or do not take the time to daub ourselves with the scents that seem to be pleasing to others in our culture. Communication also happens in the way we fill spaces. Depending on how we feel about a person, we will draw closer or farther away from him. You can spot young lovers from a distance by their proximity to one another. On the other hand, when a couple comes to our home to discuss a problem, we can often pick up the signals of their hostility toward one another simply by the way they both choose seating several feet apart.

Any pastor will tell you that some people send messages about their state of mind and soul by where they sit in a church worship service. If they feel in touch with God, they will sit close to the front. But if they are feeling spiritually cold or even rebellious but had to come to church anyway, they'll find a seat in the back of the sanctuary or up in the balcony. And when the service is concluded, they will avoid the door where the pastor is greeting people. Somehow, they equate shaking hands with the pastor with having to come to terms with God.

When someone speaks, we listen for tone of voice, volume, and speed of speaking. And we listen for silence—what is being said, and what is not being said.

GAIL: I encourage Gordon to "listen for the silences." That's when you are liable to hear the most important messages.

GORDON: You learn to look for signs in the behavior of people that are out of the ordinary in terms of their normal performance. The other day I noticed that the way an acquaintance of mine was dressed was totally out of line with his regular dressing habits. Usually he wouldn't be caught dead without every article of clothing color-coordinated. But on this occasion, he'd mixed plaids and stripes, and his colors clashed terribly. Now for many people that wouldn't and shouldn't mean a thing. But not for this man. A closer look revealed tired eyes and a sagging posture. When I took him aside and said, "You're not a happy man, are you?" he immediately broke into sobbing and poured out his heart about a terrible humiliation he was facing.

GAIL: I have had women come and tell me that a friend is probably in trouble. They'd observed the exteri-

or of the friend's house for several days and noticed that
the shades were never raised. The person in the house, it
was later discovered, had been sending out a message
about her sense of inner isolation and pain. But the
message would never have been received if someone
hadn't been reading beneath the surface.

GORDON: Sometimes we find that part of our beloved New England culture is a kind of bluff-your-way-
through mentality. It's an interesting game, if not a sad
one. It is as if some simply dare you to find out what is
really going on inside of them. We have often watched
people in severe anxiety over a failing relationship nevertheless smile and offer the glad hand to anyone they
meet. But if you were to ask them specifically about the
state of a particular relationship, they would immediately
dissolve into tears. That's one reason we have felt it even
more important to seek out the "hidden messages" people are inadvertently delivering. They'd deny it, but
they're usually hoping that someone picks up their code
and bothers to ask.

GAIL: Even a person's unwillingness to meet another's eyes has a revealing tale to tell. The eyes are
usually the mirror to the soul. You can read shame, hurt,
or joy in someone's eyes if you are concerned enough to
learn how to "read."

And, of course, we communicate with our words. The choice of
those words is very important. Words can cut like a knife, soothe like
a tender caress. Words can enthuse, discourage, open up mysteries,
and make a weak person become strong.

The sum total of all of these language forms is the sharing of
ourselves and our concerns with one another. And where that does
not happen, there is likely to be serious trouble.

When Communication Is Stifled

On the other hand, communication can be deliberately squelched
when people either by choice or neglect create an atmosphere in
which communication and fellowship become impossible. That happens in homes and offices all the time. Take the humorous account
of a moment in her home years ago described by Mrs. Billy Graham.
We smile when we read it because it could easily be matched by any
of us.

I remember one time when Bill was away. We had four children then, all terrible sleepers. I used to get up from 3 to 7 times a night. I awoke one morning looking a wreck—hair a mess, no makeup. Franklin was a baby and I didn't bother to change him; I just picked him up and plopped him in the high chair. And that morning every time Gigi, the oldest girl, started to say something, Bunny, the youngest girl, interrupted her. Finally Gigi slammed down her fork and said, "Mother, between looking at you and smelling Franklin and listening to Bunny, I'm just not hungry." I thought to myself, we Christians sometimes take away someone's appetite for the Lord by the way we live and by the way we appear and by the way we sound.[2]

Call it an appetite or an atmosphere, our obnoxious ways can make it almost impossible for anyone to communicate with us if we're not careful.

The oldest son of singer Bing Crosby, Gary, writes of the breakdown of his relationship with his father and pins it all on their inability to communicate. The father was the idol of millions of Americans for whom he crooned songs for several decades. Professionally he was a remarkable communicator. But in his home, his son writes, he was unable to express love or joy for his children in a way that they could understand what he was saying. As a result, everyone in the family suffered terribly.[3]

There are many reasons people do not find communication in personal relationships an easy matter. It is easy to blame lack of time, conflicting schedules, and much pressure. And certainly that has become a primary problem in the family, as the center of work and family life have been separated in the urban culture. A century ago, when most families worked together day and night, there was a common language, a common task, and a common need for talk of all kinds. Today that need has been seriously impaired.

Illustrating an extreme case of how unnconnected our paths can become, one woman told us, "My husband works on a highly classified project for the Defense Department. I don't have the slightest idea what he's doing ten hours per day. He can't breathe a word of it. Frequently he will be gone for several days, and I don't have the slightest idea where he is. All I have is a phone number for some Washington office if there is an emergency. They'll know where to reach him, he says."

Sometimes communication in relationships does not happen be-

2. Joan Gage, "Mrs. Billy Graham Answers Your Questions," in *For Women Only: The Fine Art of Being a Woman*, ed. Evelyn R. and J. Allan Peterson (Wheaton, Ill.: Tyndale, 1974), p. 191.
3. Gary Crosby, with Ross Firestone, *Going My Way* (Garden City, N.J.: Doubleday, 1983).

cause people have such low self-image that they believe they have nothing of value to say. Having come from a family background where their words were generally ridiculed, they have developed the habit of not saying anything that might risk ridicule, argument, or competition. They keep their feelings, their opinions, their concerns to themselves, and only the most intensive questioning will elicit any self-revelation at all.

In many relationships communication slackens because one of the parties has learned that the other will challenge anything that is said. One person may not accept criticism; or another will not allow an observation to pass without trying to match it with something better or more knowledgeable. Thus there is a degeneration of communication simply because everything seems to end up in confrontation. It doesn't take too long for the other party in the relationship to resort to increased amounts of silence.

We will not communicate with a person who squelches everything we say; nor will we communicate when our words are likely to be used against us in the future or revealed to everyone else.

GAIL: Another possible reason for the breakdown in our talking to one another has something to do with the general demeanor of a person. My husband is a man with a forceful personality. I keep on reminding him that if you could measure personality force on a scale of one to ten, he would quickly have his eyes opened about the way some people see him. When he makes a statement on what he thinks is a number two level, he needs to realize that there are some who will hear what he's said as if it were a number seven or eight, simply on the basis of their perception of who he is. That has to do not only with his personality but with the office of leadership that he holds. He sees himself as a mild person, but others may perceive him as a strong person. Thus, communication can get distorted very easily because he comes across more strongly than he intended. Fathers have to be careful about that in their relationship to their children, bosses with their subordinates, other leadership with their people.

Some men by their large physical size can adversely affect communication if the other person, physically much smaller, is intimidated by the size differential and becomes choked with fear or anxiety.

Among the many reasons that communication sometimes breaks down is a lack of perception on the part of the hearer. The disciples of our Lord often had this kind of problem. He would tell them things about Himself, about the future, about their own potential, and they simply couldn't bring themselves to internalize what He had told them.

When Jesus was about to ascend to heaven, He told the disciples, "You don't understand what I'm saying now, but some day you will." They lacked faith at times; they had contradicting personal interests at other times. Sometimes they were engulfed in fear; on other occasions they were too culturally conditioned to think of the possibilities Christ was offering them.

Certain issues in life to which a person attaches emotional significance may never get a fair hearing no matter how clear and plain the speaker may be. The great national debates going on today over nuclear power, abortion, military defense, and the protection of the environment sometimes seem so futile. Who is listening to the other? Who is persuadable any longer? Intelligent people who insist that they are rational thinkers? Not always! And it is sometimes no better inside the church in relation to some of the theological and ethical matters with which Christians need to wrestle.

ENHANCING OUR CONVERSATIONS

If we are going to achieve a high level of communication in relationships, we shall have to be able to *measure* the quality of our conversations with one another. We have to know whether or not the things we are saying are getting through and if we are communicating about subjects and reactions that enable another to know us as we should be known. At least that is the way we attacked this important issue in our marriage and family.

For us it began with a simple tool John Powell gave in one of his fine books on loving relationships.[4] He proposed that there are five levels of potential verbal communication. When we studied those levels, we immediately began to use them to study our family communication process. The results were remarkable.

LEVEL ONE

To begin with, Powell wrote about something he called the level of *cliché*. This, of course, is the simplest and most common of all the ways people communicate with one another. Clichés are more or

---

4. The references to John Powell's system of conversations come from a cross section of his talks and writings. We have borrowed Powell's concept of conversational levels and added our own comments.

less exchanges of symbols; we call them verbal algebra. A handshake, for example, is a cliché in gesture form. It suggests an extension of friendship, of greeting, and proposes that nothing of hostile intent exists between two people.

There are famous handshakes and, in some cases, famous "unhandshakes." In 1954, Chou En-lai, premier of the Peoples' Republic of China, went to Geneva to represent his government at a conference on the future of Indo-China. Entering the conference room a few minutes before the meeting was to begin, he spied John Foster Dulles, the American secretary of state, and went to greet him.

When Chou extended his hand, Dulles drew back, putting his own hand behind his back, publicly snubbing the Communist. It was a humiliating moment for Chou En Lai, and he never forgot what happened. Historians have speculated that that bit of hostile "level one" communication—on a cliché level—created a momentum that kept the Chinese and American governments out of touch for almost two decades. Years later, when there was need for diplomatic contact to settle the dispute in Viet Nam, there were no grounds for conversation between the two nations. Could it be possible that thousands died because back at the beginning one man could not respond to the "level one" gesture of another?

We use verbal clichés all the time, of course. Meet a friend in the corridor at work when there is no time to visit, and one is liable to say to the other in passing, "How're you doing?" The other responds, "Not bad; how's yourself?" "Super!" comes the reply. Perhaps both add a concluding "Have a good day!" as they disappear around the corner.

What's been said in that communication? Not a whole lot, really. At best, two people know that the other is generally all right, that they are both on speaking terms, and that they're equally busy and now is not a time to talk. All that is contained in a cliché. And that may have been all that was necessary and important to say.

Clichés are, in fact, a necessary part of a busy culture. We wouldn't have time to say all the things we'd like to say if we didn't use clichés.

We once spent some time in a country where Islam was the prevailing religion. The missionaries who were our hosts related how time consuming it was to go to market, because every person they knew would stop and engage them in endless conversation, formal greetings, questions and answers, which were part of their way of life. "How's your mother, your father, your sisters, your brother? How are the people in your village?" These questions were not only asked, but it was expected that they would be reciprocated. Much of the marketing time, the missionaries told us, was taken up in simply greeting people. Fortunately or unfortunately, in our culture we save time by resorting to clichés. Our "level one" signals shorten these exchanges to a matter of seconds. Some will not necessarily think that to be a virtue.

Obviously there are places where clichés are a virtue. But not if that is the only level of communication at which two people operate. Sometimes well-meaning Christians will operate at a cliché level with their friends. Afraid to get beneath the surface to where people really are, conversations are reduced to a theological vocabulary that can really be quite meaningless. Think of some of the things we unthinkingly say to each other.

"We're praying for you, brother." The expression may mean just that; on the other hand, it might suggest that that is all we intend to do for that person, and they should not expect anything more. (Do you remember Linus standing in front of Snoopy's doghouse in the middle of a raging blizzard exhorting a freezing Snoopy "be warmed, Snoopy, be of good cheer and be warmed!" Snoopy would much preferred to have been invited into Linus's house and given a warm bowl of puppy chow.) "The Lord really blessed us today." Possible translation: we laughed or cried a bit and generally felt very good. But the words probably mean little more than that.

"Praise God!" On some occasions words like those can be little more than a "filler" because someone couldn't think of anything else to say. Clichés can also cover embarrassing silence.

Although it is important to note that clichés are necessary and useful in our busy days, if they are as far as two or more people go in their communication—which is often the case—then there can be serious problems.

Occasionally we have taught John Powell's levels of conversation to various groups of people. And when we've done so, we've used sample conversations to illustrate what we mean by each of the levels. And although it's difficult to simulate the most natural of conversations, we used dialogues such as the following, one which has as its participants a pastor and wife. The pastor has just arrived home from Sunday school and morning worship. As he passes through the kitchen where his wife is preparing the family's dinner a conversation begins.

As you read, note how much of the exchange is purely cliché—level one conversation.

Wife: Do you realize what time it is? What took you so long to get home?

Husband: The usual stuff, I guess; only more of it. Where's the paper?

Wife: Come on, dear, the paper can wait. I want to talk to you about your impressions of the morning. How do you think things went?

Husband: It was just a typical morning; what more is there to say? I'm all talked out. Now can't I just sit down and look at the sports page?

Wife: Honey, do you realize how little you tell me about things lately? You know, it's embarrassing to me to go to some meeting and discover that some people know a lot more about what you're doing than I do.

Husband: Oh, it can't be that bad.

Wife: Oh, yeah? It's actually getting worse. Do you know how long it's been since you've actually sat down and talked with me about anything you're thinking or feeling? I'm out of touch.

Husband: You're exaggerating.

Wife: I couldn't be more truthful than I'm being with you right now. Something's got to change, dear, or this relationship of ours is going to be in trouble.

Husband: I think you're just tired from a long morning. . . .

Here is a sad exchange between two people. A woman is trying hard to reach out to her husband, to touch him. And he's proving untouchable. If she is making a misjudgment, it is probably in her timing. She's trying to get a tired man to respond, and it isn't going to work. Her attempt might work better on a Monday afternoon, and somebody will probably have to tell her that. On the other hand, he is turning her away with level-once, cliché-like statements. And if he persists in communicating with her at that level only, their relationship will take a serious turn for the worse.

> GAIL: I can tell you right now that our marriage and our friendship would never have stayed healthy if Gordon had responded like the man in that dialogue. But the fact is that there are many people in relationships—marriages and friendships—where that sort of conversation takes place repeatedly at tense moments. When I listen to those two in the dialogue, I get the feeling that the clichés are a defense mechanism set up by a man who doesn't want anyone entering his life right at that moment. Perhaps he is tired; perhaps he is worried or

preoccupied. But it's obvious that the clichés are a cover-up. He wants to get away. If only she'd waited until Monday.

LEVEL TWO

John Powell suggests that communication can happen at a second level, which he calls *facts and reports*.

At this level there is much conversation, but it is all based on the exchange of information about things beyond or external to the lives of the two people involved. This communication may center on things of mutual or momentary importance. But it lacks personal response or involvement.

Two friends discuss a ball game, or an office dispute, or a program in the village square. Spouses talk about bills, the children, or what color to paint the house. A parent talks to a child about what shirt to wear. Two church leaders confine their conversation to what went wrong with the youth program. Or a Sunday school class carefully restricts its conversation to matters of doctrine and theology even though the class may have several people who are hurting or struggling. Nevertheless, everyone may pretend that they are all right. As long as the conversation can stay on affairs external to the speakers, there is a certain amount of comfort and security. No one is unnecessarily opening himself up to where he can be known too intimately.

We've learned from talking with many married couples that, all too often, husbands and wives remain at this level for days. The relationship never grows as a result, and two people are little more than roommates in their home.

Let's pick up the dialogue between the fictional pastor and his wife, whom we left muddled in clichés, and see how it might illustrate a level-two conversation.

Husband: If you're really concerned about the sort of day I had at church, I'll tell you.

Wife: I'm listening.

Husband: When I got there this morning, all the elders were standing outside because no one had remembered to bring a key to the church. So I let us all in; we spent time in Bible study and prayer, and everyone went his own way.

Wife: Any problems with anyone?

Husband: No.

Wife: Then why did Dick Wittingham look so glum all through

the services this morning? I thought something might be wrong.

Husband: Not as far as I know. Sunday school started late as usual, and then I got down to the office to get ready for the worship service. And that's all that happened of significance this morning. There! Happy?

Wife: I suppose so, if that's all you've got to say.

Again, there is little that attracts one to a conversation of this nature. We have learned a few facts in the exchanges the two have made, but what do we know about *them?* Very little.

And that is why it is so important that we realize there are other dimensions, or levels, to the things we can say to one another. But in getting there—level three and beyond—there is increasing risk of self-disclosure. Are you ready for that?

6

The Many Levels of Talk, Part 2

John Powell's third classification of conversation is significantly deeper. It is called the level of *opinions and judgments*. And for the first time, when people talk at this level, there may be a sharing of something within the persons themselves.

What happens when we speak from the basis of our opinions is that we attach something of ourselves to our words. We become a bit more vulnerable as we throw out our own reactions to situations and circumstances. Here it is that risk begins to take effect.

It is very important that a certain amount of opinion and judgment be included in the communication between people who reach and touch. But when that happens we need to be careful. For in friendships, when one person attacks the opinions of the other with regularity, there will be a squelching of that person's mind. He/she will begin to enter a shell and probably choose no longer to speak at those deeper levels.

When we offer opinions and judgments we are bringing to our conversation the benefit of our thoughts, our convictions, our insights.

Let's return to the continuing dialogue between a pastor and wife as it moves to an even deeper level:

Husband: What did you think of the morning?
Wife: Well, I don't want to seem unduly harsh because I know

you're tired, but I think you and your people ought to think through whether or not you are really doing the adults justice in Sunday school.

Husband: Oh, come on; you're not going to start up on that again, are you?

Wife: Are you saying that you're just not interested in listening to someone else's opinion about how a program comes across?

Husband: Of course not! But you keep harping on the Sunday school program. I get tired of hearing about it.

Wife: But *you* don't have to sit through those "opening meetings" like some of us do. I'd listen if I were you.

Husband: Well, not now; I'm too tired. Besides, I'm sick of Sunday school myself right now.

The man in this conversation isn't handling himself very well at all. Is there anything good we can say for him? At least he is beginning to permit his wife to speak her mind. He may not agree with her, but a fair exchange of information is taking place.

If he is smart, he'll listen carefully and not be so defensive. His wife is offering him a judgment that is different from the perspective that he has. Whether she is totally right or not is not the issue; she has a responsibility and a right to offer something from this level. And if he wants a relationship where people are able to touch one another, he will have to listen to her.

If we replayed the conversation and softened his attitude just a bit, it could have sounded something like this:

Husband: What did you think of this morning?

Wife: I don't want to seem unduly harsh, but I think you and your people ought to think through whether or not you are really doing the adults justice in Sunday school.

Husband: Do you realize you have brought that subject up every Sunday afternoon for the last month or two? What's bothering you so much? I must not be hearing or seeing what you are.

Note how easily the conversation could change now into something from which both of them could profit. This would be an introduction to level three at its best.

LEVEL FOUR

But the levels of conversation can go and should go even deeper. Call the fourth level that of *feelings*. That is a dimension of conversation that many people in our culture rarely reach, at least on a healthy basis. Some express certain feelings in a negative way—anger in traffic, for example.

But when people express their feelings in a healthy sense, they are beginning to open up the deepest parts of their lives. They are not necessarily speaking from the authority of logic and reason, but rather they are communicating from areas of their inner lives that are often beyond words. They are talking about how their emotions, their hearts, respond to various situations.

When a person speaks at the level of feelings he is free to say, "I feel sad today," or, "I'm just plain down." It is a level where one can say, "I don't know why, but I'm scared about where all of this is leading." Still another is speaking at this level when she can say to a friend, "The whole thing just makes me very angry and hurt." "I'm feeling dissatisfied about all of this," someone says.

Positive feelings need to be expressed when people are reaching and touching:

"You know, I really like it when you're around."

"I really feel good about this project."

"A day like this brings me more happiness than I ever could imagine."

Many people are quite reluctant to express feelings. Why? For one thing most feelings cannot be defended. Feelings are not good or evil. They just are! But in many lives, people have come to the conclusion that they are safest when they keep their feelings to themselves. As children, their feelings may have been ignored, repudiated, even punished. As teenagers, their feelings may have been laughed at or gossiped about. And few things register more profoundly in the heart than a mistreatment of a person's feelings. Deep hurt or humiliation can cause people to suppress feelings so that they not only never express them to others but avoid even acknowledging their existence to themselves.

Then again, some have had the experience of having their disclosed feelings used against them at a later date. What had been opened up in confidence is brought to light at a future time when the one-time friend becomes an enemy. Occasionally, something said in a vulnerable moment comes back to haunt the speaker in a moment of conflict with another. It only has to happen a few times this way, and one becomes increasingly reluctant to deal at the feelings level ever again.

The fictional pastor and wife are dealing on a level-four, feelings level, when they continue their conversation as follows:

Wife: Do you know that when you put me off like that, I get the impression that my judgments about things are just not worth much to you?

Husband: What are you trying to say?

Wife: Tell me, have you ever thought about what it's like for me to go to church on Sunday morning and keep my ears and eyes open for things that it would be profitable for you to know about so that you can do your work more effectively? Do you know how I feel when I come back to share with you what I've been observing only to discover that you couldn't care less?

Husband: That's the way you view your morning?

Wife: That's the way it is sometimes. And when I discover that you're too busy with your sports page to respond to me, the message becomes all too plain. What I observe doesn't seem to be of importance to you at all.

Husband: I guess I've forgotten the fact that I could learn a lot from what you're seeing and hearing. I've hurt you with my disinterest, haven't I?

Wife: It would hurt me more if I didn't realize that you've been under an awful lot of pressure and that your fatigue is part of what is making you become defensive and inward.

Husband: I feel bad. I've wronged you. I need to ask your forgiveness.

Wife: You're forgiven. Oh, and by the way—I really shouldn't have brought all of this up when you are so tired. So I have to apologize too.

Husband: That's all right. Now, what was that about Sunday school?

Just in time, the husband tuned in to this conversation at the right level. He discovered that he'd deeply hurt his wife, and, fortunately, he didn't ridicule or ignore her feelings. There is definite communication—reaching and touching—going on here in this dialogue because two people are expressing what they feel inside and are hearing what the other is saying.

When we hear someone express himself at this level, our response should not necessarily be: "That's a bad feeling," or, "That's a good feeling." But rather the question ought to be: "How can I best offer companionship to the one who has expressed himself in such a way?" Does he need encouragement? To be left alone for a while? Does he need someone to laugh with him, to cry with him? Does he merely need to be listened to? At a feeling level there is little need for *answers;* there is just a great need to be *heard* and for the person expressing such feelings to *know* he's been heard.

LEVEL FIVE

The deepest of Powell's levels of communication we call *maximum truth*. Here at level five truth is spoken and heard in its most candid, but helpful, form.

When we communicate with friends, children, or spouses at this level we are more than likely dealing with exchanges like affirmation or rebuke, confession or forgiveness. Here dreams and disillusionments are revealed. Relatively few relationships reach this level with frequence.

Affirmation is that exchange of communication where a person shares with another about potentials and possibilities he has seen in the other. In a sense, when we affirm others we are believing in their present value and their future potential. We have seen their performance, and we want them to know that we place value upon it. We all desperately need this form of conversation. Goethe once said: "When we treat man as he is, we make him worse than he is. When we treat him as if he already were what he potentially could be, we make him what he should be."

William Barclay tells how Benjamin West began his trek toward becoming a great painter. Affirmation was the key.

> One day his mother went out leaving him in charge of his little sister, Sally. In his mother's absence he discovered some bottles of colored ink and began to paint Sally's portrait. In doing so he made a considerable mess of things with ink blots all over. His mother came back. She saw the mess but said nothing. She picked up the piece of paper and saw the drawing, "Why," she said, "it's Sally!" and she stooped and kissed him. Ever after Benjamin West used to say, "My mother's kiss made me a painter."[1]

Our words of affirmation to one another can be the "kiss" that motivates growth and development, self-worth and desire. We grow best in an environment in which there are those who believe in us and are unashamed to communicate that belief.

> GORDON: As I look back through my life, I am caused to realize that I am the product of a chain of "affirmers," men and women who believed in me, who took time to communicate to me their conviction that God had something in store for me in serving Him.

1. William Barclay, *Ephesians, The Daily Study Bible,* 18 vols. (Philadelphia: Westminster, 1976), p. 178.

> Many times I think I would have quit, dropped out, if it
> hadn't been that there was some key person who believed
> in me.

A father communicates affirming words to a daughter who struggles with her sense of strangeness as she enters puberty. A friend
affirms another as she struggles with the demands of a new job. A
wife affirms a husband who is learning how to take care of tasks
around the home. Affirmation is one of the deepest levels of communication there is. All of us need it, and relatively few are usually
willing to give it.

It is interesting to note that at critical times during His earthly
ministry, Jesus Christ was affirmed by His heavenly Father. Coming
out of the water of the Jordan River where He had been baptized,
Christ heard the voice of God: "This is my Son, whom I love; with
him I am well pleased" (Matthew 3:17). On the Mount of Transfig-
uration, He was again affirmed by the Father in front of others.
There was a sense in which He needed the reminder that the Father
was pleased with Him. And perhaps the chief agony on the cross was
that Jesus sensed the strange absence of the Father as He bore the
sins of humankind. You could say that His great pain was the loss of
the momentary experience of His Father's affirmation.

But *rebuke* is also a serious part of this fifth communication level.
Unfortunately, rebuke is seldom done properly. In the biblical sense,
a rebuke means to confront a person with the consequences of poor
choices. The rebuker matches another's performance against the
laws of God because he has become temporarily blind to what is
happening.

When King Ahab of the Old Testament saw a piece of property
that he very badly wanted to own, he made an offer on it. The owner,
Naboth, refused, saying he wasn't in a mood to sell. Ahab returned
to his palace and began to sulk. He literally went to his bed and
turned his face to the wall and wept. It was a perfect time for rebuke
from a wife, who should have pointed out the absurdity of his
childlike reactions.

But Jezebel didn't communicate at the right level. She joined his
mood and in fact congratulated him for his feelings by setting into
motion events that ultimately took the life of Naboth and gained the
property for Ahab. That was a case where the lack of a rebuke did
more to ruin the lives of two men than anything else.

Paul loved the Corinthians, although it is sometimes difficult to
understand why. He loved them enough to rebuke them with force.

"I wrote you out of great distress and anguish of heart . . ." he said, "not to grieve you but to let you know the depth of my love for you" (2 Corinthians 2:4). Paul loved that congregation too much to allow it to collapse for want of communication on this fifth level.

When you read Paul's rebukes to the church at Corinth, it becomes clear that he administered rebuke because he valued the long-term relationship he wanted to have with them. He was willing to accept the pain of their potential temporary negative reaction that might occur because he knew that it would pay off in the end. But there was no doubt that the rebuke was a very painful one for the Corinthians to receive and for Paul to give.

A loving rebuke is a part of any meaningful relationship. Its intensity depends upon the intensity of the relationship. Naturally it is not in our purview to go about rebuking everyone we know. Rebukes are exchanged between good friends who have proved care and concern for one another, between mentors and their followers where there has been a history of credibility and faithfulness; between a parent and a child; between spouses. A rebuke is not merely an angry expostulation; it is a expression of loving concern that something in the life of another is going wrong.

Among many Christians there is plenty of criticism and gossip, but there are relatively few who are skillful at rebuke. Often we allow good friends and associates to move toward some form of personal destruction because we are afraid to confront them with the truth. Not to rebuke is a tragedy in a relationship.

Of course some will not accept rebuke. There is little reason to rebuke a person who is defensive and unyielding. We have all seen the person who bristles with anger at the slightest indication of disagreement or confrontation. In the need to be touched, we must ask ourselves continually, "Am I willing to accept rebuke by those who live in the primary circle of my relationships?"

In the days of John Adams and Thomas Jefferson there was a period when their relationship fell into great, seemingly unresolvable conflict. It seemed nothing would bring them to reconciliation. One day Dr. Benjamin Rush, a fellow signer of the Declaration of Independence, wrote to Adams beseeching him to heal the breach between the two men.

It was a loving rebuke of sorts. Rush faced Adams with the open sore of the relationship, and, at first, Adams put up a strong protest of innocence:

> Why do you make so much about nothing? Of what use can it be for Jefferson and me to exchange letters? I have nothing to say to him, but

to wish him an easy journey to heaven, when he goes, which I wish may be delayed, as long as life shall be agreeable to him. And he can have nothing to say to me, but to bid me make haste and be ready. Time and chance, however, or possibly design, may produce ere long a letter between us.[2]

But Adams was more willing to accept rebuke than he first appeared. And although he seemed to strongly resist Benjamin Rush's rebuke, he nevertheless wrote to Jefferson six days later, and their friendship—dormant for almost eight years—was restored.

GORDON: Philip Armstrong, the late director of the Far Eastern Gospel Crusade, was a friend who knew when and how to confront with the truth. Several years ago Phil and I were traveling together, and I said something about another person that was terribly unkind. I suspect most people, even if they didn't agree with my comment, would have allowed it to pass by. But not Phil Armstrong. He loved me too much and probably reasoned that he didn't want me making such a fool of myself on other occasions when my friends might not be so kind. So he said, "Gordon, your comment is really unkind and unjust. It's not the sort of thing a man of God should be heard saying."

I learned that day something about what the old mystics called the governance of tongue. One doesn't have in a lifetime too many friends like Phil, who are willing to confront for the sake of another's growth. That painful moment has saved me from many other destructive moments I might have got myself into.

On this fifth level, people find the ability not only to affirm and rebuke but also to *confess* and *forgive*. One feels the freedom in certain relationships to say a genuine "I'm sorry; I blew it!" And another feels free to say, "I forgive you." Those are hard words for some, and more than one friendship has been cooled down because one of the parties in the relationship, having offended the other, was unable to face up to his insensitivity and acknowledge it with a confession of wrong doing.

"He just finds it impossible to say, 'I'm sorry,'" someone says

2. Dorothie Bobbe, *Abigail Adams* (New York: Putnam, 1966), pp. 321-22.

about another. But the inability to deal with confession means that relationships of all sorts will be restricted. Confession and forgiveness mean that short accounts are being kept in a relationship. Proud people who find that impossible allow accounts to go on longer and longer and get bigger and bigger. Finally, the relationship can no longer take the weight of so many unresolved hurts, and it breaks down.

Paul Rees, in writing a brief biography of John William Fletcher, a great Methodist preacher in the days of John Wesley, tells of a day when another clergyman, Thomas Reader, read one of Fletcher's books and became so incensed that he immediately began a three-days journey to the author's home to tell him off.

> On arrival at the vicarage, he knocked loudly on the door. To the servant who answered the knock he presented his request for an interview with the vicar. No sooner had the servant announced the gentleman's name than Fletcher, recognizing it, hastened from his study to receive the visitor, and spreading out his hands, he exclaimed, "Come in, come in, thou blessed of the Lord! Am I so honored as to receive a visit from so esteemed a servant of my master? Let's have a little prayer while refreshments are getting ready."
>
> Mr. Reader was so puzzled, taken aback, overcome. Although he spent three days in the vicarage, he was unable to muster enough courage to even broach the subject that had been seething in his heart. He later testified that "he never enjoyed three days of such spiritual and profitable intercourse in all his life."[3]

What a remarkable forgiving spirit Fletcher revealed. And because he was such a man, note how the relationship between himself and one who could have become a bitter enemy became a thing of intense friendship and growth.

At this fifth level of communication one is also free in certain relationships to speak of *dreams* and *disillusionments*. It is a special relationship indeed when we are able to open our deepest desires and struggles to another and know that our words will be carefully weighed and appreciated.

The fictional pastor and wife that we invented can operate on this fifth level also. Let's watch them take their conversation one step deeper. Remember how they began? One trying to reach; the other avoiding the touch? Remember the harsh words? Note the difference now in a conversation that is on the fifth and deepest level.

3. Paul Rees, "Life of John William Fletcher." Speech given at John Fletcher College.

GAIL: My husband has always been a dreamer of sorts. When we were first married, I quickly discovered that I tended to be the realist and he the idealist. In the early days when he would share some of the dreams he had, I was tempted to want to bring him back to solid ground. But I quickly learned that there is a place, a time, and a relationship where a man or woman should feel free to paint his dreams out loud. If I could not share mine with him and if he could not share his with me, wouldn't there be a temptation to find someone else who would listen? Perhaps if no one was interested, he might have stopped dreaming altogether.

Husband: You know, when I came home I was really in an ugly mood. I wasn't quite truthful with you when I said that it had been a typical morning.

Wife: What do you mean?

Husband: That elders' meeting that I went to didn't really go so well.

Wife: Well, I thought you seemed awfully preoccupied when I saw you in your study. What happened?

Husband: It just hit me this morning that there are several people on the board that I'm not in touch with these days. And this morning when we talked before prayer, I thought I was picking up some feelings of distance—like I was not on their wavelength.

Wife: Is it something you think you can do anything about?

Husband: I'm not sure yet; but it leaves a guy with a feeling of nervousness in the pit of the stomach.

Wife: Perhaps you need to face the fact that you've been ignoring some of those elders. They want to be with you, and you've allowed yourself to get too busy with other things.

Husband: Oh, I don't know.

Wife: Don't you now? You're as aware as I am that you were hurt by some of the things they said to you at the last elders' meeting. You didn't like it when they talked about the length of your sermons.

Husband: Well, yeah.

Wife: And it's been a bit hard for you to face them, hasn't it? You're hurt, and so you want to just stay out of their way until you can resolve it.

Husband: I suppose you're right. I've been putting off thinking about what really went on in that meeting.

Wife: Honey, that's not like you. Normally, you resolve things quite quickly in your mind. A lot of us aren't as good about that sort of thing as you are. I've sensed for some time that this one has gotten to you. Now, don't you think it's time to do something about it?

Husband: Are my feelings that obvious?

Wife: I couldn't miss them.

Husband: All right; I'll get in touch with some of the elders tomorrow.

Wife: That's more like the man I know. I'm proud that you could face the truth about this. There're not many men that are able to do it as gracefully as you do, you know.

Husband: Not many men have the sort of relationship that we do where you can speak your mind without blowing a guy out of the water. That's what is so special about you.

When two or more people find ways to talk to one another at such levels, marvelous things can happen. Not every conversation takes place at the deepest levels. Healthy communication means an ability to move up and down among the levels as time passes.

When communication is established in a relationship, it provides a base for strength when crisis comes. What some do not understand is that if that base has not been established before there is stress or pressure, the relationship will most likely break down when crisis comes.

Philip Yancey writes of John and Claudia Claxton, who found themselves battling with her Hodgkin's disease, and the possibility that death was imminent. When Yancey visited with them and tried to analyze what was at the root of the strength of their relationship, John Claxton, a chaplain's assistant in a hospital, told him this:

> I have seen dying patients in hospitals. It's not like on the TV shows or in the movies like *Airport*. In the movies, couples who have fought for years, in the face of danger, suddenly forget their differences and come together. Life doesn't work that way, however,
> When a couple meets a crisis, the result is a caricature of what's already there in their relationship. We happened to deeply love each other and had open communication. Therefore the crisis drove us to each other. We were unified and we trusted each other. Feelings of blame and anger against each other did not creep in. The crisis of Claudia's illness merely brought to the surface and magnified feelings already present.[4]

4. Philip Yancey, *Where Is God When It Hurts?* (Grand Rapids: Zondervan, 1977), pp. 154-55.

That strong witness to a relationship under fire through illness is what communication is all about. Simply put, those who reach and touch know how to talk and be heard. They understand the importance of regular communication that scans the levels at every opportunity.

They talk directly, over the phone, through cards and notes, and in a hundred other ways that make possible a constant flow of information about the partners in the relationship.

And they know how to listen when the other talks. They keep an open ear and a wide eye to take in every nuance of information at every level. And when they've heard, they respond with appropriate action.

It is no different when we are talking about a friendship or a marriage; the principle is the same. Those who reach and touch *communicate*. And that is what the brilliant composer and conductor Mahler never learned to do. And that is also why a young aspiring composer left his presence a crushed man. But a John William Fletcher knew how to communicate loving acceptance to a hostile visitor. Mahler turned a friend into an enemy, whereas Fletcher turned an enemy into a friend. The difference began with communication.

7

When Communication Seems to Sour

The story is told of a man who was being pursued by a roaring, hungry lion. Feeling the animal's hot breath upon the back of his neck and knowing that time was short, he cried out in desperation, "O Lord, please make this lion a Christian."

Within seconds the fleeing man was aware that the lion had stopped. And when he looked behind him, he found the lion kneeling, lips moving in obvious prayer. Greatly relieved at this turn of events and desirous of joining the lion in meditation, he approached the beast. And when he was near enough he heard the lion praying, "Bless, O Lord, this food for which we are exceedingly grateful."

There is a dangerous tendency to suppose that Christian relationships must be devoid of all conflict—that if people are followers of Christ, all will be peace and tranquillity.

That was the impression of one Christian businessman who enthusiastically revealed one day his high hopes for a partnership he had just created with another Christian. "I know it is just going to be tremendous for us," he said. "This relationship won't have any of the problems I normally have. Why, do you know that we even pray together before we begin our meetings?"

It wasn't long before the two partners were on the verge of litigation in the courts because they could not resolve their problems in spite of the prayer before each meeting. Their first difficulty? Assuming that Christians never conflict.

No relationship will last long without conflict, including those involving Christians. Conflict is a part of communication that is inevitable. And to the extent that we are thinking people with values, convictions, perspectives, and feelings, all of us are going to find ourselves in disagreement with others on various occasions. The fact is that all conflict is not necessarily wrong but can be a track toward personal and relational growth.

The Bible is full of the stories of disputes between good people. How they resolve those disagreements with one another provides an interesting primer on the subject of conflict in relationships. Can you imagine the disciples conflicting with Jesus? The fact is that they did.

Conflict brewed the day that Peter disagreed with Jesus over the course of the future and the Lord's announcement that He would die at the hands of His enemies. Jesus' reaction was a loving but harsh one. Conflict existed the day that the impatient disciples attempted to stop small children from being brought to Jesus for blessing. Jesus sharply reversed their action.

Do you recall the dramatic storm scene on Lake Galilee? What else can it be called but angry conflict when the disciples surrounded the sleeping figure of Christ, accusing Him of not caring for their terrifying situation. "Don't you care if we die?" they screamed. Later there would be conflict over what should be done to take care of 5,000 people who had pursued Jesus into the wilderness area. Jesus said they should be fed; the disciples thought they should be sent away.

There was conflict when the disciples argued among themselves over who was the greatest; and there was conflict when they argued over the reports of Christ's resurrection.

Again, it's important to recognize, when one studies relationships, the tendency to suppose that good people with good intentions do not conflict. But history actually demonstrates the opposite. When one studies the relationships of Christians in the book of Acts—the history book of the early church—there emerges a startling amount of material on the subject of conflict. In fact it would be easy to gain the impression that conflict was the normal life-style of the early Christians.

We can understand why, if we think about it for very long. For example, Christians often bring to all kinds of relationships a highly defined agenda. A Christian marriage involves two people who are earnest in bringing the best God has to offer into their home. They are not going to be without opinions about how that is done.

Friends are going to have an agenda for relationships that is more than just the pursuit of fun and amusement. And when people move beyond that level of activity, there will be a not infrequent clash of opinions as to where energies and resources ought to be invested.

Furthermore, the church tends to draw people who like to reduce life to principles and laws. These are people who want answers to the great moral and ethical dilemmas of our day. They want to face up to the problem of sin and evil and know what to do about it. This intensity is inevitably going to create an atmosphere ripe for conflict as they compare and contrast their insights with others.

Let us not forget that the Christian family is marked with people who have brought into the fellowship their own brokenness and personal weakness. They admit to that fact when they acknowledge the need of a Savior. Thus, issues of personal life are more likely to be discussed and faced than in other, secular organizations. In Christian relationships there can be a tendency to confront actions and attitudes that non-Christians would either avoid or ignore, or simply criticize or gossip about. In Christian relationships, conflict is likely to arise because there is a tendency to believe that these things ought to be confronted and healed.

Conflict often arises among Christians because of the stress and pressure of constant change. In the community of faith, lives are changing through growth or spiritual rebellion; circumstances are changing about us, and assignments to Christian service are changing. Since few of us accept or face change very easily, the effect can frequently be seen in the way we take our anxiety and frustration out on one another if we are not sensitive to what is actually happening to us.

Perhaps the greatest reason for conflict still lies in the fact that we are sinners, and—as we have seen earlier—that makes it less likely that we will be fully sensitive to the way others think or what they care about. We are prone to selfishness, greed, covetousness, and anger unless we keep a vigilant guard upon ourselves. And things like those, unwatched, become a breeding ground for conflict in any relationship.

It is helpful to study the conflicts of the early Christians in the New Testament—helpful because they appear to have faced the same basic issues we live with in our relationships. Nothing basic seems to have changed. But more than that, it is useful to note their conflicts because we can learn something from the good and bad ways in which they resolved their struggles and what happened as a result.

Take, for example, the first conflict that appears in the book of Acts (chapter 1). The congregation had to resort to an election to solve a problem. Someone had to take the place of Judas Iscariot as one of the apostolic leaders. Who was it to be?

There is no indication of anger, but the fact is clear that there were two candidates put up by people who had differing views as to who the new man ought to be. So an elective process of sorts was utilized in order to determine the mind of the Holy Spirit.

What is admirable about the problem-solution is the fact that when the process was completed and Matthias chosen, there is no indication of any further debate over the matter. The issue was closed. Election was the solution to the conflict, and it was resolved peaceably as far as we can tell. Everyone was satisfied, apparently even the man who was not selected.

Then conflict arose between Peter, the pastoral leader of the church, and Ananias and Sapphira, two people who attempted to spiritually defraud the congregation by pretending they were something that they actually were not (Acts 5). Peter's confrontation of the couple seems quite harsh and the punishment extreme—they were struck dead by the Holy Spirit. In fact, it actually appears as if the Holy Spirit took the solution out of Peter's hands. We can only assume that the seriousness of their deceit was not something the embryonic church could afford to absorb at that time.

The first major conflict in the early church appears in Acts 6. Christian Jews of Hellenistic cultural origin protested that the Christian Jews of the Judean area were discriminating against their widows and orphans. It is obvious that everyone was giving generously to the support of the needy in the congregation, but the issue appears to center on the fact that the generosity of the people was being poorly administered. We do not know if the accusation included charges of gross or purposeful negligence or whether it was merely a protest over the ineptness of the organization's leaders.

But the important thing is that the conflict was confronted, brought to a solution pleasing to all concerned, and when it was over its results brought further growth to the congregation. The account is a remarkable model of conflict at its best and ought to be studied carefully when people ponder conflict in relationships.

Rather than become defensive at the criticism against their leadership, the apostles wisely handled the conflict by first surfacing it, not permitting it to remain at the "murmur" stage where it could have been destructive. They acknowledged that there was indeed a genuine case to be made, and the hint appears that they realized that they were simply the victims of a clash of priorities.

To the credit of the aggrieved, they do not appear to have pressed their accusations but rather to have participated in the resolution of the problem. All engaged in the selection of spiritual men who would take the administration of the funds from the shoulders of the apostles. If there is a key to the solution of the problem it is this: The Hellenistic Jews had a just cause but were originally in danger of handling it poorly. They were murmuring. But the Judean Jews, who seem to have been the root of the wrong, pursued the right solution. The result? The church grew. Conflict properly handled often makes growth happen: in marriages, in friendships, and, surprising to say, in congregations.

Later there was conflict between Peter and the elders of the church (Acts 11), when word reached Jerusalem that Peter had not only successfully preached to Gentiles and brought them to faith but had actually accepted hospitality in a Gentile home. This was an unheard of thing for a Jew to do (Christian or non-Christian).

Again, the confrontation between the parties who were in disagreement is worth close study. The men caught in dispute examined the facts with open minds and hearts. If there was any hostility in their encounter, it was because they all were facing new realities and insights that went against the grain of all their traditions. But the facts reigned supreme in their thinking, and when the evidence of God's hand had been clearly presented and evaluated, conciliation quickly followed.

Acts 15 gives us the record of another significant conflict, one that could have split the early church wide open. This time the facts were disputed, and personal opinions that were in bold contrast did surface.

The resolution? A compromise—one with which everyone could live but still remain reasonably faithful to their convictions. If there is something to be learned about conflict in Acts 15, it is that well-meaning Christians with strong beliefs found that compromise was more important at that point than endlessly dividing from one another and creating a debilitating weakness to their fellowship and witness.

But on the other hand there seems to have been no possible compromise in the aftermath of the Jerusalem council of Acts 15, when Paul and Barnabas argued over including John Mark in their proposed second missionary journey. Here the only resolution appears to have been the going of their separate ways, which is exactly what they did. At least it can be safely said that their conflict did not destroy or discredit either of the two men.

There is one more major conflict in the book of Acts, and it features Paul in opposition to a large number of Christians over his decisions to press on to Jerusalem (Acts 21). They begged and cajoled him not to go, but to no avail. He was resolute, and he won. Both groups thought they knew God's will. But Paul's stubbornness won out, and only history can judge who was right.

It's important to examine these ancient illustrations, which come from our Christian roots. They should be reassuring to us in the sense that they tell us that very little in human relationships is really new. But now that we have centuries of perspective, we can look back on those illustrations and learn much from them that can be applied to marriages, friendships, and life in the congregation.

What can we learn from those biblical conflicts? Probably several lessons and principles. Let's list them.

1. In the best of the conflicts, *each side genuinely respected the opinions and judgments of the other.* Thus, they stuck to the issue.

All of us have seen and been part of conflicts where parties disagreeing with one another quickly drifted from the real issue to begin attacking one another. In such affairs, one's reputation, one's motives, one's own esteem may be called into question. There can be name-calling and accusation, resulting in unrestrained anger. It is not unusual for people to begin to forget what the original purpose of the conflict was because so many other matters have insinuated themselves into the confrontations.

But when well-meaning people choose to respect one another, then they can vigorously exchange views—all toward an objective of discovering the greatest amount of truth in the situation. They are careful to make sure that only the issue itself stands between them.

2. *The relationship was more important than someone's beating another.* Or put another way, in a Christian relationship there are no winners or losers; there are only "growers." From the conflicts in Acts, one gets the clear impression that the believers were most anxious to resolve problems in such a way that everyone would profit from the solutions. No one had to humiliate or intimidate another.

That is a very important matter for us to consider. It is a key issue in many marriages and friendships if someone always feels a need to be vindicated, always has to feel triumphant in order to maintain a sense of self-esteem. There are those among us who do not feel free to admit to wrong at any point in a conflict. It would be too damaging to our sense of personhood. Thus we tend to enter into conflict with a do-or-die fervor. We are liable to find ourselves much more anxious to win than to get at the truth. And that is destructive to persons and relationships.

3. *There was a willingness to compromise when necessary.* That makes some Christians uncomfortable, if compromise has been scorned as the way of the faithless.

But, like it or not, we must look at the relationships in the Jerusalem council of Acts 15 and agree that a compromise was the root of the resolution. Leaders listened carefully to the experiences and insights of Paul and Barnabas. But they were also sensitive to the concerns of the traditionalists from Jerusalem who had serious problems with the way Gentiles were being admitted to the Christian church. And while the compromise seems to have leaned heavily toward Paul's opinions and judgments, it nevertheless reflected the feelings and concerns of the other side.

The biblical record does not indicate how well everyone accepted the compromise. But we do know that there was a reasonable peace among the brothers of the faith after the dispute was settled and that Paul did his best to give support and aid to those very same people when they faced stress and struggle in a time of famine and persecution.

We can learn something important from the Jerusalem council. There will be many disputes where an obvious answer to the problem is simply not forthcoming—at least not one that pleases all parties, who are honestly expressing themselves. A compromise on an issue therefore becomes important. Compromise gives time for all involved to test the issue further and search for deeper insights and truths. We should not always be afraid of this sort of solution.

4. *Unresolved conflicts will fall into the wrong hands.* If two people who are in conflict with one another cannot bring their problem to a resolution within a reasonable amount of time, it is certain that others will become involved.

That seems to have been Paul's great concern when he wrote to the Philippians and urged Euodia and Syntyche—two Christian women—to resolve their problems quickly. He was obviously concerned that their friction would become a cause that others might join.

That sort of thing happens frequently in relationships. Children quickly begin to pick up the "vibrations" when their parents cannot resolve a conflict. A congregation suffers when some of its leaders begin to resist one another. Younger or less mature Christians begin to debate the issues, start to take sides, and often permit the debate to get out of hand. That has been the most frequent source of church divisions. Among a group of single adults, two people can fall into disagreement and before long the atmosphere is so poisoned that everyone is hurt.

5. *Anger has no place in conflict* except to provide energy toward finding out the truth. All of us have seen the man or woman who has a temper. We've also seen how often that person "wins" conflicts, because almost everyone else is terrified of seeing that anger ignited.

Angry people make a search for truth and growth in a relationship nearly impossible because others, perhaps out of self-perservation, become more interested in keeping the "lid" on than in expressing their perspectives and positions. Men and women who cannot control their anger rarely ever find out what others are thinking. No one has the courage to risk an outburst by telling the truth. Life can become very lonely under such conditions.

When a person knows that he has a temper, he must be very careful to make sure that he has it under control. Not to be certain of this forfeits that person's right to be heard in conflicts. He must not be permitted to destroy other people through intimidation of that sort.

6. *There is a kernel of truth in virtually every point made in conflict.* We must learn to look and listen for it. In conflict people often express feelings, opinions, and judgments that they would otherwise never have made known. Much of this is good. And others have to learn to watch for such expressions. When truth surfaces in conflict, it can become very valuable if we know how to handle it.

One looks at the Barnabas/Paul division. It is easy to gain the impression that Barnabas normally backed down to Paul's stronger personality, and that is probably what frequently happened while they were traveling on their first missionary journey.

But something happened when John Mark became an issue be-tween them. The normally flexible Barnabas suddenly dug in his heels and wouldn't budge. Was Paul wrong? We know only that many years later Paul would write to Timothy and ask him to bring Mark along to Rome because he was a "profitable" man. Perhaps if Paul had taken note of Barnabas's conviction on the issue of Mark the first time around, he might not have made the decision he did to leave the young man behind.

7. *Confession and forgiveness are an indispensable part of the resolution of conflicts.* We pressed this principle upon our children at the earliest age. Our son, Mark, found it hard to admit that he was wrong, and we used to worry that perhaps he lacked a certain freedom to face up to his own weaknesses. As a young boy he found it difficult to lose in a game, to admit that he didn't have all the facts in a discussion, or that he'd made a mistake when we confronted him with something we believed was wrong.

We doubled our efforts at modeling confession and forgiveness in front of him. We almost made a game of it. If one of us made an error in something, we often exaggerated the matter, going to the most absurd extremes to point out how wrong we knew ourselves to be. These moments, of course, often ended up in lots of family laughter. But little by little Mark got the point. It was all right to be wrong, and it was even better to acknowledge it.

There came a day when we no longer worried about Mark's having a problem at all in this area. Now he knew how to handle a loss of a game or a bad day of performance in his athletic life. And now he knew how to acknowledge that his viewpoint might be deficient at one point or another. I'm glad we attacked it when he was young, however. I see a lot of parents who do not spot this problem until it is too late.

GORDON: We did work hard at this, not only in the family but in all of our friendships. We learned that keeping short accounts of conflict in all relationships is very important. I work with a staff of ten associates plus many more in our support staff at Grace Chapel. Although we work together in Christian ministry, that is no guarantee (as we saw in Acts) that there is not going to be conflict.

Long ago, I had to learn how to resolve conflicts. When I make a mistake or a misjudgment I have had to learn to go to the right man or woman and say, "I want you to know how sorry I am." Occasionally, I inadvertently offend some in the congregation with an offhand remark or even by ignoring them. Usually they manage to let me know, and I suspect that it is often a moment of test just to see how much I care. It's important for them to see their pastor able to admit that he made a mistake. A proper apology or confession can help everyone grow. That goes for managers, for teachers, for parents, and for anyone else who wants health in relationships.

Of course the corresponding response to confession is forgiveness. And forgiveness implies our decision not to hold something against another—perhaps even if they have not yet apologized.

The forgiving life-style is essential to healthy relationships. It simply has to happen, and where it does not there is sickness.

We have had countless conversations with hurting people where the subject matter sprang from the problem of forgiveness.

The pain one lives with when he has been unable to forgive a parent for past hurts—or when one spouse has held a past problem against the other for years! Trust and confidence erode; freedom and joy dissolve under the heaviness of the unresolved relationships. We have seen two friends have an argument and one of them lack any ability at all to forgive the other. Literally, years have passed with little more than a "hello" between them. Why? One carries resentment and hostility because he cannot forgive.

8. *When conflicts are handled properly, everyone grows.* Insights are exchanged; truth is discovered; we learn more about one another and what is truly important. For more than anything else, conflict reveals what is deep within us: what we care about most of all, what has hurt us, what we believe in. As these sorts of subjects boil to the surface, relationships advance in their quality and ability to help us to grow.

The man who prayed that the lion chasing him would turn out to be a Christian misunderstood something important. Being a follower of Christ does not preclude conflict (the early church is proof of that). Rather, being a follower of Christ should make a supreme difference in how one handles conflict.

When true Christians conflict, they are simply communicating at the deepest possible levels. And if they do it as if Christ were watching, the conflict can turn into a growth experience. The fact is that Christ is always watching.

8

Growing a Person, Part 1

Our favorite picture of our two children is one taken when Mark was six years of age and Kristen was three. In it they stand side by side. Mark has a firm, determined grip on Kristy's hand, conveying the impression that he has everything under control. He seems to be saying that he is prepared to handle any difficulty that might come Kristy's way.

We weren't aware that the picture ever had any special meaning for Mark, now in his twenties, until we sat recently in a seminary lecture hall and listened to him speak to a group of graduate students about the quality of life in a pastor's home. When quizzed about brother and sister relationships, he alluded to the picture and described it to the students. Then he said, "The only regret I have about my relationship to my sister is that I kind of wish I'd held her hand more like that while she was growing up."

It was Mark's way of reflecting upon a principle of relationship that has been very important in our home and in our friendships. We call it *enabling*. And even though Mark would wistfully tell a group that he wished he'd held his sister's hand more the truth is that he did a more than adequate job.

To be sure we weren't always sure that that was what he had in mind when, as a child, he would beat her mercilessly in games only boys should play. But even there he built into Kristy a sort of healthy toughness that comes in handy today when she copes with her teenage society. Later, when the children entered the busy social whirl of adolescence, it was of great comfort to us as we saw him take her into his circle of friends and help her build credibility with the crowd. He certainly held her hand and introduced her to growth.

The Son of God had a form of this enabling principle in mind when He called upon the disciples to love one another as He'd loved them. They themselves were the products of His enabling ministry. Enabling has to do with the investment people in a relationship make in one another. It is what happens when we concern ourselves with the question Is the person with whom we are friends, spouses, or family a *growing* person because we have touched him? What sort of contribution have we made to his maturation?

When you take a quick look backwards to those men who later became apostles of the Christian church, the transformation of their lives over a period of just a few years is nothing short of remarkable. And that transformation was largely due to their relationship to Jesus Christ, particularly in the case of Simon Peter. It was a long distance, growth-wise, from working as a fisherman on Galilee to becoming a missionary-apostle in Jerusalem and other parts of the world. But he managed it under the enabling influence of Christ in a way that can be a model for all relationships.

How did Jesus enable Peter to emerge as the man we ultimately know him to be? It all began, of course, with a commitment made by the Lord: "Follow me, *and I will make you . . .*" (italics added). And Peter, like the others, accepted the invitation and chose to follow. The transformation of the fisherman took place as he watched Jesus closely. And what he saw was the result of Christ's *transparency.* Additionally there was the Lord's *sensitivity* to who Peter was, where he needed to grow, what his weaknesses were, and what he could become. Jesus knew Peter fully and well and looked far into his life, much further than anyone else had ever bothered to look. And, of course, there was *communication,* as Peter expressed important insights and information during his time of growth in discipleship.

But one more important element must be added to this overview. And that is what we're calling *enabling.* What were those factors in Peter's life with the Savior that made it possible for him to grow and to become the finished product that we see during the apostolic age? What did Jesus do in His relationship to Peter that made the difference?

Simply put, He enabled him. He poured into Peter some qualities of spirit and performance that made a dramatic transformation. And He did that not through force-feeding, threats, or conditions. He did it by creating a unique environment, an enabling environment, in which Peter could freely grow to the maturity of apostleship, God's special purpose for his life.

The Bible teaches that God has a special purpose for every person. Each of us is absolutely unique; each of us is endowed with an unusual constellation of gifts and capacities, insights and observations. But it is likely that many of us do not fully appreciate what that means. We need assistance in order to grow to the fullness of God's purpose for ourselves. And that is the ultimate design of a relationship: we are meant to participate in the bringing of each other to maturity. *We enable each other to grow.*

Exactly how does that happen in friendships, in families, in marriages, and in any other kind of human relationship? Let's set forth a metaphor that may provide the best insight on enabling.

When it is gardening time each spring, the man or woman with a green thumb first goes out to prepare the soil. It is turned over, mixed perhaps with some fertilizer, and carefully marked off for the introduction of seeds and plants. The gardener is generous with time, energy, and resources. And as the weeks pass, he does everything possible to protect the resultant growth.

He knows when the tomato plants will need to be staked, what the beans and the peas will need in terms of sunlight, and how much room cucumbers will need in order to spread out. Weeds will be dealt with; sneaky animals seeking an early unearned harvest will be fenced out; and insects will be resisted by just the right kind of pesticide. Each day the gardener will enter the garden in an "enabling" mood. And if the job has been done correctly, each growing thing will reach its full ripening or greening at the right moment.

Good gardeners know that you cannot cause such growth. You can only contribute to it. And so they work hard to create an enabling environment, one in which the plants in the garden are released to become whatever they are designed to be. Gardeners are content to plant, to nourish and protect. The plants of the garden must grow for themselves.

And that is exactly what we are pursuing in relationships when we talk about enabling one another to grow. We can certainly see this relational principle in the friendship between Jesus and Peter. When the two met, the result was dramatic growth for the future apostle. And how that happened may give insight into how we help one another in all of our relationships to grow in similar patterns.

The enabling environment in which Peter grew was charged with grace. Was Christ ever more gracious with anyone than He was with Peter? When someone acts toward another "graciously," he is choosing to give that person *what he needs, not what he deserves*. Few people needed that sort of relationship more than Peter. He was impetuous, impulsive, and abrasive. It took a lot of grace to enable him to grow.

What are some of the marks of grace in a relationship? Where were they seen in the experience of Jesus and Peter? Comparing their situation with that of the metaphor of the gardener, let us suggest that the first mark was patience.

ENABLING ONE ANOTHER DEMANDS PATIENCE

In human relationships, people who enable others are always, first of all, *patient* people, and patience is a quality of character that often seems to be in short supply in this modern world. Patience is something that seems best understood in an agricultural world where people are used to giving growing things time to mature. They've learned that they have no choice in the matter.

But in a world where computers, supersonic jets, and satellite communications create a sense of instancy, we can lose the meaning of patience; we simply don't like to wait for things—or for growth and development in people. We want each other to change, to mature, to respond in certain ways instantly. The one with whom a person is most likely to be impatient is himself. But sometimes it takes years to develop wisdom, the grace, and the endurance we want to see in one another. Such people-growth (like plant-growth) cannot happen outside the environment of patience.

Simply put, patience is the willingness to generously give another time and space to grow. Patience means we withdraw *our* expectations, *our* timetables, *our* methods, and permit God's to prevail. Patience does not demand; it waits. Our friend Dr. David Seamands tells of a woman who once acknowledged that her impatience with her immature husband had often caused her to act as if it was God's responsibility to love him while she changed him. But she later learned that "it was my job to love him and let God change him."

Jesus Christ was extremely patient not only with Peter but with all of His disciples. When many of us would have been tempted to write off the disciples because of their frequent stubbornness and resistance to truth, Jesus stuck with them, giving them the time to grow.

He did not overreact to their panic in the boat when the storm became treacherous. Nor did He publicly embarrass them when they failed to give assistance to a father with a demon-possessed boy. And Jesus was not needlessly exasperated when the disciples failed to show their belief in Him when He challenged them to feed the 5,000. Rather, He always directed their attention to the issue involved and away from any attack on their personhood.

Patience is the lubricant in relationships, one could say. It is what stops "heat" from building up when someone we know begins to rub us the wrong way. When there is stress in a relationship, patient people do not immediately lash out. Rather they first ask themselves, *How is he/she seeing this issue? Why would one choose to say or do things that way? What causes such anger, or hurt, or enthusiasm?*

We are showing patience when we act in sensitivity and attempt to monitor the stress periods and blind spots of others. If we understand what it is that they do not see or something of the pressures that they are facing, then perhaps we will come to a new and better interpretation of their performance in a certain situation.

> GORDON: When we were a bit younger in our pastoral ministry, I remember Gail's giving special attention to a couple of high school girls in our congregation. Because she saw potential in them, she met with them on a weekly basis for some time. One of the girls tested Gail's patience with regularity. She might make the weekly meeting, but then again she might not. And she struggled with her faithfulness to God. Many, many times Gail would say to me, "Sometimes I feel as if I'm really wasting my time with her. She's just not that interested. Why bother?" And then she would go back to the starting line with the girl again. But Gail's willingness to accept a young, immature teenager who had potential and who could grow eventually paid off. Today, she is the wife of a fine pastor, an excellent mother, and a spiritual leader in her circle of friends.

How often each of us has silently begged for the mercy of others in the circle of our relationships. We want to cry out, "If you knew how tired I am, how pressured I feel, how much hurt there is in my heart, how dumb I feel." We want to ask people for the luxury of patience with us. But our tendency is, when someone else in our relational world acts poorly, not to think first about the possibility that they also may be under great stress.

Many times a person has no idea that he is creating the impressions or inconveniences that he is. We say he has blind spots. And until the proper moment comes for him to find out, we will be called upon to show patience and give him room to grow.

By no means is patience *compliance*. It is not that we are simply ignoring another's immaturity or irresponsible behavior. Rather, it is a matter of knowing that every one of us has a personal growing season.

David the psalmist took great comfort in his relationship with God, for he felt reassured that God was looking over him like a father who "has compassion on his children . . . for he knows how we are framed." David felt secure in the relational patience of his heavenly Father because he knew that God was not expecting more of him than he was capable of giving at that point in his growth process.

GORDON: Few verses in the Scripture meant more to me in my young spiritual life than David's assertion in Psalm 103 that God is patient with our development. I suddenly realized that I never wanted my children to be anything more than what was mature for any given age. When our daughter was twelve, I delighted in her normal behavior as a twelve-year-old. I would have been alarmed if she'd tried to act like or seize the privileges of an adult. I'd have applied discipline only if she'd acted like a six-year-old. It occurred to me that God was patient with me in the same way. He wasn't expecting spiritual performance from me that was out of line with the years I'd been walking with Him. He knew my frame—just how much stress it could take. His patience helped me relax and stop comparing myself with other Christians who were ahead or behind me.

GAIL: I think it's important to emphasize that this patience begins with ourselves—giving ourselves room and time to grow. Our church family recently lost a lovely young woman who died suddenly. She had been a radiant person, pushing hard to grow into a mature Christian. But she was also patient with herself. I have a copy of one of her diary entries in which she commits herself to an austere diet. She resolves to cut out all between-meal snacks *except* on Thursdays and Sundays. Somehow that amuses me, because it suggests that Becky understood herself and was going to make reasonable allowances for the "human" in her. In the first phase of her diet, she'd cheat on her diet only on two days of the week.

Can you imagine the patience demanded of Jesus on those days when His disciples (after considerable time with Him) came on three successive occasions with petty attitudes and proposals. They wanted to know who among them was to be considered the best (something of a power struggle). They wanted to get His compliance on their decision to tell a non-disciple to stop delivering people from demons (something of exclusivity). And they wanted His permission to destroy a small town by fire from heaven when they were refused hospitality (a spirit of vengeance). Why put up with men like that? Answer: Jesus saw the future; He knew what they were to become, and that caused Him to be gracious and patient with their momentary childishness. He stuck with them.

In his book on spiritual leadership, J. Oswald Sanders notes a revealing comment by J. Hudson Taylor concerning his relationship to the men and women around him who often seemed to slow him down rather than make his way easier: "My greatest temptation is to lose my temper over the slackness and inefficiency so disappointing in those on whom I depended. It is no use to lose my temper—only kindness. But oh, it is such a trial."[1]

Difficult as it may have been, Taylor did keep his temper; he was patient with those who were not traveling at the speed or in the direction that God was leading him. And without such an element of graciousness, the people around him would never have grown and been enabled to carry on the Taylor vision long after he was gone. Every relationship in our world needs patience like that, even if it is painful at first.

ENABLING ONE ANOTHER DEMANDS PROTECTION

In an enabling relationship, patience has to be augmented with another quality of grace. We have come to call it *protection*. In that family picture that means so much to us, Mark holds Kristen's hand, and he steps just a bit in front of her, extending his other hand outward as if to ward off anything that might come in their way. His seems to be a protective posture, as if to say that he'll break the way.

When you look at Jesus' friendship with the twelve you can see all sorts of occasions where He stepped in and offered a word or mounted an effort that prevented them from facing the full consequences of silly mistakes or immature choices. If He hadn't protected them on occasion, they would probably never have made it to the scene of the crucifixion, certainly not beyond that point.

From our vantage point, knowing the end from the beginning, we

1. J. Oswald Sanders, *Spiritual Leadership* (Chicago: Moody, 1980), p. 99.

can see how Jesus was constantly breaking the trail in front of the men who followed Him, and for Peter particularly. Few of the disciples needed protection more. He was in completely new territory.

Peter could manage a fishing boat and a seafood business without too much trouble. But confronting evil, healing people, and preaching the kingdom—that was another story. Although he was definitely drawn to the task Jesus laid before him, he nevertheless seems to have managed to make every classic mistake that could have been made. He badly needed protection from his own compulsions and from the consequences of his frequent blunders.

Healthy human relationships require mutual protection. Paul employed the word *forbearance,* one that carries the sense not only of protection but also shelter. We see constant examples of this need for shelter or protection in the behavior of small children. You are drawn to a lovely little child standing at its mother's side, and you kneel and try to coax it to come to you. But instead of doing so, it may in fact withdraw and wrap its arms around Mother's leg. It seeks a shelter in the folds of her dress and protection in the touch of her body.

To differing extents, that sort of protection or shelter is an indispensable element of every relationship. We must shelter one another. That is exactly what Jesus did with Peter on many occasions. If Christ had not protected His friend during this growth process, Peter probably would have (to use a modern idiom) shot himself in the foot.

Take the time, for example, when Peter proposed a walk on the water with Jesus (Matthew 14:28). Everything was going fine until Peter became impressed with his own agility. Immediately he began to sink. It was the hand of Christ that pulled him back up. Many of us might have been tempted to allow Peter to sink a little deeper and choke a bit. Not Jesus. He pulled him up instantly and walked with him to the boat.

That's one view of protective grace: the extension of the steadying, helping hand. Paul had this sort of grace in mind when he wrote to the Galatian Christians about a "sinking experience" that every one of us has faced at one time or another: "If someone is caught in a sin, you who are spiritual should restore him gently" (Galatians 6:1).

In enabling relationships a good friend is sensitive to the places where a brother or sister is liable to weaken and "sink." He/she concentrates on being ready to offer the steadying hand.

In the case of the Galatian situation, Paul was concerned about people who might have committed serious moral or ethical errors. The usual reaction in many relationships would have been to dismiss such people from the congregation or simply to begin ignoring them, dropping them from one's life. But Paul calls for protective restoration—a hand that would lift such sinking persons.

A protective, steadying hand may have to be given when someone is in bigger trouble than he can personally handle. We have seen examples of this when people go through the tragedy of a family or marital breakup. A woman who recently experienced a divorce told us: "When a person loses a spouse through death, the Christian community seems to run to them with things to do to keep them busy in their grief. But if you lose your spouse through divorce—no matter what the circumstances—the Christian community seems to run in the other direction and actually deny you things to do to deal with your grief."

The person who loses a job will often discover that people will offer condolence and support for a few weeks, but as time passes actually withdraw more and more, leaving that person alone just at the time when a hand is needed the most. "I guess I just don't know what to say to him when I see him coming," someone says in trying to explain the neglect. Perhaps there are times when words are less important than just the quiet hand that pulls one out of the sinking condition.

We have a vivid memory of the only major emergency our family has ever experienced. Our infant daughter had been rushed to the hospital because she had mistakenly taken a drink of turpentine. Some of the medical personnel who worked on her thought we might lose her. We felt as if we were sinking to the bottom as we sat there in the waiting room absolutely helpless. We shall never forget the sudden bouyancy we felt when several men and women from our congregation came to sit with us. Their presence was the hand of Jesus to us in our sinking state. They had no answers to give, nor did they have any way of making the situation more promising. All they had was that steadying hand that offered protection from fear and dread.

The protection of Jesus over Peter was never more evident than on the night of His betrayal and crucifixion. In front of all the other disciples Peter was prepared to stand and pledge his ultimate love for Christ. He was ready to die for the Lord if necessary. Of all those in the group, only Jesus knew how futile were Peter's words, how inadequate his will, how soon the promise would be broken.

It would have been the human thing in a relationship for Jesus to have ridiculed or at least ignored Peter that night. But rather, Jesus had a gentle warning of what was about to happen: "Simon, Simon, behold, Satan demanded to have you, that he might sift you like wheat, but I have prayed for you that your faith may not fail; and when you have turned again, strengthen your brethren" (Luke 22:31, RSV).

But Peter persisted: "Lord, I am ready to go with you to prison and to death."

And Jesus' sad response: "I tell you, Peter, the cock will not crow this day, until you three times deny that you know me."

Protection bonded with patience produces love like that which Jesus showed for Peter that night. It seemed the right moment for someone to have said, "Peter, you've had three years to come to your senses and three years to face up to your impulsive mouth, but here you go again. We're going to have to find someone else with better character and quality."

But Jesus didn't; and that is the kind of love He was calling the disciples to show for one another in the years to come. You have to believe that Peter often looked back on that evening and was awe-struck at the magnanimity of the Savior.

Jesus was actually trying to protect Peter from himself. He was touching him with a firm warning as to what would happen. As we see the Lord trying to get Peter's attention we are reminded of one of the Peanuts cartoons in which Linus once found Lucy in one of her crabby moods. Then he saw Charlie Brown headed in their direction and knew that the two of them were apt to bring out the worst in each other.

A lesser person than Linus might have been tempted to stand back and enjoy the fireworks. After all, if Lucy and Charlie got into another one of their brawls, Linus could have stood on the sidelines congratulating himself on how much self-control he had in contrast to both of them.

But we all know that is not Linus's protective nature. And so he stopped Charlie and said, "When Lucy's crabby like this, everybody should be warned to stay away from her." Then to Charlie's amaze-ment, Linus went to where Lucy was sitting in silence with "crabbi-ness" written all over her scowling face and began to surround her with emergency road flares. It was Linus's way of protecting Charlie and others from needlessly experiencing Lucy's wrath during one of her bad moments. But at the same time Linus was protecting Lucy from revealing a side of herself that needed correction. He stuck with her when others would have walked out of her life.

Jesus stuck with Peter at his worst moment; Paul says to stick with stumbling Christians; the Bible calls for us to offer steadying hands to struggling, vulnerable people in our world.

One of our nineteenth-century heroes is Charles Simeon, vicar of the Holy Trinity Church in Cambridge, England. He once said:

> I consider love as wealth; and as I would resist a man who should come to rob my house, so would I a man who would weaken my regard for any human being. I consider, too, that persons are cast into different moulds; and that to ask myself, what should I do in that person's situation, is not a just mode of judging. I must not expect a man that is naturally cold and reserved to act as one that is naturally warm and affectionate; and *I think it a great evil that people do not make more allowances for each other in this particular.*[2] (Italics added)

Jesus made enormous allowances for Peter that night, knowing that in just a matter of weeks this beaten man would become a powerful preacher in Jerusalem through the fullness of the Holy Spirit. That night Jesus enabled Peter to carry on toward that destiny by protecting him from the folly of his momentary weaknesses. Patience and protection: without these elements in a relationship, we will never learn the joy of being growing persons.

2. Hugh E. Hopkins, *Charles Simeon of Cambridge* (Grand Rapids: Eerdmans, 1977), p. 134.

9

Growing a Person, Part 2

When we look at that special picture of our two children, we see Mark's one hand grasping Kristy while the other reaches forward as if to protect. Some day he would realize that there is another direction for a hand to reach: upward!

THE ENABLING RELATIONSHIP DEMANDS INTERCESSION

Relationships that enable persons to grow have to be marked with intercession, the effort of prayer one makes on behalf of another. Intercession is the act of standing between someone and God in order to bring them together. That was what Jesus had in mind on that crisis-laden night when He said to Peter, "I have prayed for you." Peter seems often to have been the object of intercessory prayer.

As a leader of the church, Peter found himself in prison one night, when the enemies of the congregation were trying to stamp out its leadership. "But earnest prayer for him was made to God by the church." The story of the answer to that intercession is among the most thrilling, if not amusing, in all of the Bible. Before the prayer meeting ended, Peter was miraculously released from prison and stood pounding on the door of the very place where prayer was being offered. The intercessors were incredulous when they opened the door and found him standing there. It was intercession of great effect.

All relationships will be relatively shallow until intercession enters the enabling environment. We must learn how to hold up one another before God.

The most magnificent example of intercession in relationships is seen in Jesus' great prayer for the disciples in John 17.

> I do not pray that thou shouldst take them out of the world, but that thou shouldst keep them from the evil one. . . . Sanctify them in the truth. . . . I do not pray for these only, but also for those who believe in me through their word, that they may all be one. . . . Father, I desire that they also, whom thou hast given me, may be with me where I am, to behold my glory which thou has given me in thy love for me. . . . I made known to them thy name, and I will make it known, that the love with which thou hast loved me may be in them. (Verses 15-26, RSV)

Here is a model of intercession. The concerns of Jesus Christ when He prayed for His friends were that they would know victory, unity, and joy; that they would experience protection from the enemy; that they would appreciate the holiness of their special tasks and be properly equipped to undertake them.

How many friends do any of us have whose prayers we can count on? Probably not too many. Perhaps we could enlarge that number if we initiated the element of prayer in our friendships, our marriages, our families. The keeping of prayer lists, the checking up with regularity to see how God may be answering prayer are all parts of the building up of a relationship.

> GAIL: One of the special things I've discovered that deepens a friendship is to make sure that I follow through on a promise to pray. When I commit myself to intercede for people, I put their names in my journal and pray for them everyday. But with regularity I do two things beyond just praying. I check every time I see them to find out how they're doing and how I can perhaps even sharpen up the prayer request. And, second, I drop them an occasional note, not only saying that I'm continuing to pray but even adding a fully written out portion of Scripture and perhaps a few sentences of the kind of prayer I'm praying. Gordon and I have found that people are deeply moved by such extensions of enabling. Intercession builds relationships, to be sure.
>
> GORDON: I remember being in a group one day when someone made a hostile comment about someone

> who was absent from the gathering. Immediately, some-
> one else spoke up and said, "Before we say anything else,
> let's pray for that person." The gossip ceased as of that
> second.

We have seen a remarkable difference in relationships when two
or more people decide to make intercession a significant part of
their lives. They agreed upon particular issues of growth or challenge that would be regularly brought before the Lord. When possible there was prayer together, and at other times there was simply
the promise of a regular intercessory effort when they were apart.

Some find that a hard thing to do. Men, for example, sometimes
admit that praying with their wives is very difficult for them to
initiate. Why? Perhaps it has something to do with the fact that
praying triggers a recognition of personal weakness, something that
men often find hard to deal with. Having been culturally trained
never to admit weakness, something within fights the entire notion
of praying with others.

On the other hand, women find it relatively simple to acknowledge weakness, and perhaps that is why they find it easier to turn to
intercession as an important part of a relationship.

If we are to enable one another, our knowledge of what needs
prayer in the life of another is an indispensable part of the process.

The Enabling Environment Demands Forgiveness

When we talk about the "grace environment" as part of enabling
in relationships, we need to recognize another element that Jesus
provided for His disciples beyond patience, protection, and intercession. And that was *forgiveness*. Without it, no relationship can last
for very long. All too frequently, that is the great missing element in
many marriages, families, and friendships.

Time and again we have known people in Christian circles who
thought themselves to be mature people because they had studied
the Scriptures completely and took strong stands on particular convictions. But at the same time they violated what may have been one
of the most important of Jesus' principles in relationships: the ability
to forgive those who offended the relationship.

Early in His public ministry Jesus made forgiveness a major issue.
He was thinking about it when He talked of the state of heart and
mind one brings to worship. He warned His listeners never to come
to the altar of worship until they had scanned every personal relationship to insure that all conflicts had been resolved (Matthew 5:23-
24). That included the granting of forgiveness. It is obvious that

there was no place for any hint of bitterness or resentment at the altar as far as the Son of God was concerned.

But judging by performance, a lot of Christ's followers do not believe that He was serious. For it is not unusual for one to see men and women coming to worship with their marriages in a state of brokenness. Nor is it unusual to take note of Christians sitting not far from one another in a sanctuary, who haven't spoken for long periods of time due to conflict. The person who carries a force of anger within against a parent, a former business partner, or a leader that has let him down is not a rare individual. To be candid, many people do not seem to believe in the importance of forgiveness as a key to healthy, enabling relationships.

Jesus not only taught forgiveness, He modeled it. After the night of their embarrassing betrayal of Jesus, there were for the disciples three days of total gloom. And that gloom might have continued had it not been for the resurrection. The good news was that He was alive; the potentially bad news might have been how Christ would respond to their pathetic loss of courage on the night before the crucifixion. But among the very first words sent from the risen Savior to the disciples were: "Go tell the disciples *and* Peter . . ." Jesus was still talking to Peter.

Not long afterwards there was the emotional reunion on the shore of Galilee (John 21). The depressed Peter and the others had spent a fruitless (or fishless) night on the lake, and when day broke, there on the shore they saw the figure of Jesus beckoning them to a breakfast He'd cooked for them. It was forgiveness in word and deed. As the men gathered around that fire on what must have been a chilly morning, the message was obvious: the Savior had chosen not to hold against them their dismal performance in the hour of maximum danger.

Think of it: the Son of God's cooking breakfast for forgiven men. It was a magnificent picture of a healed relationship.

Forgiveness means to deliberately choose not to hold something against another when an injury to the relationship has occurred. Some used to say that forgiving is forgetting. But that is a rather frustrating principle, since most of us are too human to totally forget. It is more accurate to say that although we may not have completely forgotten, we have, on the other hand, chosen not to respond in a way that the other person deserves, but rather to give what is needed—mercy.

Forgiveness is not only an act in relationships; it becomes a style of relationship. The act becomes a style as we learn in our process of maturing not to quickly react when someone does something that offends or hurts us. We begin to take on the attitude Jesus assumed at the cross when He prayed, "Father forgive them; they're ignorant of what they are doing."

GORDON: It is very hard for some of us to forgive, especially if someone has hurt us in a most vulnerable part of our lives. On a couple of occasions in my adult life people have done something to me that seemed extremely unjust and dishonorable. My instinct should have been toward immediate forgiveness, but it wasn't. I can remember once having a feeling of such bitterness against a person that I would lie awake at night trying to think how I could retaliate, gain vengeance, and to suitably humiliate the other person as I felt I'd been humiliated.

Little by little the effect of my bitter spirit piled up. I was preoccupied with what I now know was nothing but hate. It affected all other relationships to a certain extent. It certainly hindered my walk with God. As a result I was unalterably tied to my past and the pain that that relationship had brought to me. And it began to diminish my ability to lead in ministry.

I remember crying out in desperation to God for deliverance from such a bitter spirit. The answer did not seem to come easily. Then one afternoon as I sat in the back seat of an airliner headed toward a speaking engagement, God gave me the victory I was seeking. As I acknowledged that I was guilty of hate and needed release, the freedom to forgive came. But I had to relinquish all right to get back at the person involved. I had to drop the matter in my mind. I had to promise the Lord that I would never talk about the person or the particular issue in an attempt to vindicate myself.

I'll never forget the moments that followed that surrender. It was if God cut a hole in my heart, and I seemed to physically feel hate draining out of my chest cavity. When the plane touched down I felt ten pounds lighter, and I went on to a weekend of speaking that was as powerful an experience as I have ever had. But forgiveness was the key; without it, I would have been in serious trouble.

Jesus assumed that the actions of many of the angry people were done in blindness and ignorance. He chose not to react toward His enemies but rather to show regard for the evil that was in their hearts to instigate such an injustice. That was the style of Jesus all the way through His public life. If He showed anger, it was never toward a person but rather at the sin within that caused a person to act the way that he did. To be able to separate the sin from the sinner is the first step toward being able to live in constant forgiveness of one another.

In an insightful article on forgiveness, Lewis Smedes gives further insight on how both the act and the style of forgiveness can be pursued in order to maintain an environment of grace.[1] He suggests that there are three things that need to be kept in mind.

First, he writes, when we are wronged we must frankly face the effect of what has happened. If we have been hurt, let us admit the fact to ourselves. Joseph of Egypt was wronged by his brothers on several occasions. But later when he met them as prime minister of Egypt, he showed that he had faced up to their actions and chosen not to hold it against them. "You intended to harm me," he told them "but God intended it for good." And that closed the books as far as Joseph was concerned.

Joseph wasn't unrealistic about what had happened. He had experienced all the possible consequences of their jealousy and anger. But having faced it, he was ready to get on with life.

Smedes suggests a *second* aspect of forgiveness as an act of spiritual surgery upon ourselves. In forgiving we determine to slice away the wrong act someone has done and, at the same time, recreate in our minds a new view of the wrongdoer as if he had never done the original deed. That is a courageous thing to do, and it demands the power of Christ at work in us. It is in fact what Jesus Christ was doing in the prayer of forgiveness on the cross. He was seeing those people through forgiving eyes, as if they had never perpetrated the act of crucifixion at all.

Then Smedes proposes, *third,* that he who would forgive "starts over." Reconciliation is a personal reunion of two people who were alienated but belong together. It is not excusing the wrong, nor even forgetting it. But it is choosing to free oneself from the past and look to the future.

And that is exactly what becoming a forgiving person makes possible. The one who forgives is released from the past, freed to seize the present and the future. What is sadder than the person who carries a

1. Lewis Smedes, "Forgiveness: The Power to Change the Past," *Christianity Today,* 7 January 1983, pp. 22-26.

load of bitterness and self-pity from wrongs done to him in the past? Though he may be a talented, attractive person, he rarely engages in relationships that could be called enabling relationships because his unforgiving mind is too much upon himself and the connections of the past. In fact he is nailed to the past. And no one grows in the presence of such a resentful man or woman.

Paul was cruelly beaten and imprisoned in Philippi. He had every human reason not to want to ever return to the town or, for that matter, to have anything to do with the Philippian jailer who'd made his life miserable. But because he could forgive by putting the past behind him, a church was raised up in that community that became his favorite. The Philippian Christians were enabled to grow in relationship to Paul because he followed what would become the Smedes formula of forgiveness.

Some of us possess temperaments that do not lend themselves to this style of forgiving. We hold grudges easily and for long periods of time. We instinctively want to win conflicts, justify or protect ourselves, and resent it when we lose. We may carry pockets of volcanic anger within, which are set off any time we are reminded of issues and struggles of the past. And no marriage, family, or other quality relationship can exist as long as these tendencies go unconfronted and unresolved.

Although it may be a dramatic spiritual and emotional challenge, those of us possessing such tendencies must face up to the reality of our unforgiving spirits if we ever hope to be part of a gracious environment in which others can grow.

GAIL: There is a woman in our congregation whom Gordon and I have known for more than ten years. When we first met her, she was going through the most difficult moments of her life. Her husband was in the process of leaving her for another woman. She had to face the fact that she was going to be left with two young boys, little if any financial income, and lots of loneliness.

My earliest impressions of her are of a person who appeared to be far too mild and weak to survive the pounding she was going to have to take as a single parent. I can remember the awful sadness as I went with her to court when her divorce decree was finalized. More than once we wept together over the frustration of financial resources, behavior problems, and questions of the future. There were times when she wondered if she could handle the growth process of two boys who were feeling their own kind of pain caused by their father's seeming rejection of the family.

But one of the things that kept her going was her ability to forgive her ex-husband. She followed Lewis Smedes's recipe for forgiveness completely. She did face up to the pain that was in her life but refused to grant herself needless pity, much less seek it from others. She also took a look at her ex-husband and mentally managed to separate him from his sin. She saw him as a sad and misguided man rather than someone out to hurt her, and that meant that there was never any attempt to slander him before others for the purpose of giving him a bad name.

Finally, she kept in her mind a picture of what this man could be if he ever came to a realization of the way he was running from God and his responsibilities. All of that caused her to maintain a style of forgiveness that marked both her and her boys' lives.

For ten years we have watched her maintain that style. Today both sons are young adults and are maturing into men who are her delight. And although she must continue to taste moments of loneliness and inner pain, her ability to forgive has saved her from being a bitter and unhappy woman. Her choice to live that style of forgiveness has paid off in the kind of person she is today and what her sons are becoming. Their home has been a gracious, enabling environment. Forgiveness was practiced there.

The Enabling Environment Demands Investment

When our son, Mark, turned sixteen, he began to drive. And it wasn't more than a few days later that he approached his father with the question of using our pickup truck—our family car—for a big Friday evening date.

What complicated the question was not only his relative inexperience as a driver, but also the fact that the date was to happen in the heart of Boston. Add to that the discovery that the drive into the city would be made at peak rush hour.

"Son, let me think about your question for a couple of hours and then get back to you," his father said. We talked about it and decided that, although there would be two nervous parents throughout the evening in question, it was time to trust his judgment. But his father had an idea that might put everyone's mind to rest.

Two hours later father and son talked again. "I've decided that you can use the truck on Friday," Gordon said, "but there has to be one condition."

"What's that, Dad?" Mark asked, obviously ready to agree to anything.

"I want to drive the entire route of the date with you the night before at the same time. And what's more, I want you to demonstrate to me that you know how to handle any situation you might face the next evening."

"No problem, Dad," Mark responded.

And so on Thursday night Mark and his Dad started driving north on Boston's Route 128 to pick up the intersecting I-93, which would take them into the heart of the city.

Traffic was moving slowly when Gordon suddenly said to Mark, "Son, you have a flat front tire. Did you know that?"

"No, I don't, Dad," Mark answered. "There's nothing wrong."

"You didn't hear me, Bud; you've got a flat tire because I said so. Now let's move over and change it."

When they were parked on the side of the freeway, Gordon got out and sat on the guardrail. Mark came around and said, "What do you want me to do?"

"I guess I'd want you to do whatever is necessary in order to change a flat tire," Gordon said. "You'd better get started; it looks like rain."

Shaking his head in consternation because the front tire looked just fine, Mark crawled under the truck to find the spare tire and jack. A few minutes later he crawled back out from the rear of the pickup and said, "Dad, where's the jack?"

"I'm not here, son," Gordon responded. "You may have a problem."

Mark continued to look—under the truck, behind the seat, under the seat. For ten minutes he searched for a jack he'd never bothered to locate before. Finally he found it under the hood, and before long he had the front of the truck up in the air. It was then that Gordon suddenly pronounced the tire whole again, and they started toward Boston once more.

When the two reached the exit ramp Mark was to take, Gordon suddenly informed him that the ramp was closed due to construction. "No, it isn't," Mark said.

"I just closed it," came back the reply.

And so Mark had to find another way to reach his destination without benefit of map or directions. When he did, they parked the truck in the parking lot and then immediately exited, much to the surprise of the lot attendant.

On the way home an alternator seemed to strangely malfunction, and the two men pulled over to the side to discuss what one would do in such a situation. And when they reached home and the end of the road test, both had lots to laugh about.

But the next evening when Mark left on his big date, he drove off confidently. He had been enabled. He knew how well he could perform in any untoward situation, and he knew he enjoyed the confidence of his father. In practice he had proved himself, and both he and his father knew what he could do.

A relationship in which people are enabled flows like this. The elder leads the younger, the stronger assists the weaker, the expert teaches the novice, the experienced shares with the first-timer. One pours into the other the knowledge and the confidence that are necessary for maturity and effectiveness. It is an investment of sorts: *a transfer of resources that results in growth.*

Little by little, Jesus invested in His disciples. In the early stages of their relationship He simply allowed them to watch. Then He might ask them what they had learned. It was not long before He was asking them questions, making them think. And then there came the time for experimental performances. When they returned, He would quiz them closely, making necessary corrections and suggestions.

And what was the aim of all that? The day when He could give His mission of world-evangelization over to them. He not only expected to give it to them, but He looked forward to the fact that they would do greater works and accomplish more than He had. That would be the payoff to His investment.

In terms of enabling, doing that may be the most difficult thing we have facing us in relationships—giving our best to others and then watching them move out ahead to accomplish what we've helped them to learn—perhaps even better than we can do it. This is the essence of what some call discipleship.

GORDON: One of my most special memories of my father comes from the day he taught me to ski. We took the rope tow to the top of the practice slope. When we got ready to go down the hill, he had me position myself between his skis. And down the hill we went, very slowly, of course. His hands were on my hips, guiding me along, teaching me how to lean and make the proper turns. When necessary his knees pressed against mine showing me how to properly bend and swivel. By literally being pressed against his body, I picked up the natural movements of skiing quite quickly. With each right movement he would shout encouragement, and at the bottom of the hill he would tell me what I did correctly and incorrectly. As we went down the hill again and again, I could feel him letting me drift progressively farther from him. Then came the sudden moment when he released me to ski ahead while he stopped and cheered.

Sure, left to myself I soon fell. But we started again, and it wasn't long until I was totally on my own—skiing crudely, but nevertheless skiing. Not too many days later, I was skiing with my father on the expert slopes, keeping up with him, thoroughly enjoying myself. That's the way we enable one another: guidance, constant affirmation, and final release.

Enabling relationships are marked with a willingness to give and receive guidance just as was seen in the friendship between Christ and the twelve. That they were willing to learn is just as important as the fact that Jesus was willing to teach. Conversely, enabling will never happen when one party in a relationship assumes that he has nothing to learn from the other.

GAIL: I think one of the keys to the friendship Gordon and I have experienced within the context of our marriage is the fact that we have chosen to draw guidance from one another. Perhaps my contribution to him has been one of helping him develop his people skills. On the other hand, he has taught me how to study the Scriptures and teach. I think both of us have often sat back in pride watching the other in certain situations do exactly what we'd taught the other to do. We've both grown through this process.

GORDON: On the other hand, we've seen far too many men and women in relational situations where one person assumes that the other has no investment to make. In our counseling with some Christian leaders who've failed, we've both been impressed with how often

> the one who'd failed could not take the investment of
> advice, criticism, or guidance from a wife or good people
> who surrounded him. Why do some men and women
> think that they know everything? That no one can teach
> them anything? That they can get along without the
> investment of others?

Affirmation is the second investment we make in one another if
the relationship is to be called an enabling one.

Earlier we saw an example of affirmation between the heavenly
Father and Jesus ("This is my beloved son in whom I am well
pleased"). There are many such examples of affirmation given by the
Lord to those who follow Him.

Jesus was quick to affirm Peter when he spoke boldly concerning
whom he thought Jesus to be ("The Christ, the Son of the living
God"). Mary of Bethany was affirmed for choosing the priority of
sitting at the feet of Christ, and Zacchaeus was publicly affirmed
when he recognized and repudiated his formerly corrupt activities at
the tax office in Jericho.

As we've seen, affirmation is that act of identifying and ascribing
value to things that others have done or become. Few things in the
enabling environment are more critical to growth. We see countless
examples of people who carry hurt and anger with them throughout
a lifetime because they lack affirmation at critical times in their
lives.

A delightful book, which has become a recent best seller in the
Western world, is called *The One Minute Manager.* In it a young
aspiring businessman seeks out models of managerial style that
would set him on the pathway to success. Finally, he is put in touch
with a man not far away who grants him an interview. Before long he
is being invited to tour the company and talk with people who work
for the young man's host. They share with him the key to the
successful managerial style of the company. One of the essential
ingredients: "one minute praisings."

"What is a one-minute praising?" he asks. "Catch people doing
something right," one person says to him. A one-minute manager,
he is told, touches people, looks them straight in the eye, and tells
them succinctly what was good about what they have accomplished
and how delighted management is as a result. People will do almost
anything to receive a one-minute praising.[2]

2. Kenneth Blanchard and Spencer Johnson, *One Minute Manager* (New York: Mor-
row, 1982), p. 41.

The One Minute Manager simply reflects a very obvious truth about enabling relationships. People grow by affirmation, by praisings. Perhaps it is a shadow of the praising we hope, as did Paul, to hear from God when we appear before Him some day. We all crave some significant individual to ascribe value to our person, our performance, our growth.

All relationships thrive on affirmation: marriage, parent-child relationships, and of course friendships of various sorts. And where someone resists providing it, the relationship begins to hurt and probably will not grow to the fullness of its potential.

We work hard at affirmation, especially through the sending of notes and cards. Whenever we see someone who is making a contribution of some sort that may go unrecognized, we try to make a point of praising that person through a thank-you note or even a special word when others are present and can hear the expression of appreciation.

Recently, a couple hundred of us gathered for a dinner to honor Milton Friesen, a man who has given many years to mission work in the city of Boston. He has been very sick recently, and we wanted to make sure that he knew how much we all loved and appreciated him should anything happen that would deny us that opportunity later on. Person after person came to the front to talk about things this man did to show the love of Christ among the street people of Boston.

One comment we will never forget came from a woman who sings classical music. Mr. Friesen had asked her to come to Kingston House, his mission, to give a concert for the men and women who come in off the streets to receive a meal and a place to sleep. He specifically asked her, she told us, to make sure that she sang some heavy classical music. "They are God's children," Friesen told her, "And I want them to hear the very best kinds of music possible." Her subsequent concert was Milton Freisen's way of ascribing value to his beloved street people. He is that kind of man—always seeking to affirm in creative ways.

When most people make investments, they gleefully hoard what the businessperson calls the ROI (return on investment). That is not so, however, in the kind of investment one makes in enabling relationships. For when we enable one another, our investment is ultimately designed to give the ROI away. In other words, *that which we build in the lives of other persons we finally release; we give it away.* And that is a third aspect of our investment program in growing people.

Parents invest in their children and then release them. In a strange sense friends build in one another's lives, releasing each to the service and possibilities to which God has called them.

The opposite of release is possessiveness. And nothing is more ugly than a possessive relationship, where someone attempts to hold on to another. Growth is stifled; love turns into resentment, freedom into entrapment.

Although the disciples were never more servants than the day Christ ascended to heaven, they were nevertheless released, freed to an even larger mission: world evangelization. Jesus had poured Himself into them through commitment, transparency, sensitivity, communication, and investments of all sorts. Now He set them free to make choices to follow the Holy Spirit and preach the gospel, carrying on His redemptive mission.

And that once motley group of men who had been a strange mixture of sub-cultures, vocations, and political and social groupings became the apostles of the Christian church. They changed the world. They were loved into a relationship with Christ, and they duplicated that love for one another and then subsequently to others.

Sometimes it is painful to release one another. So many of us have our own little insecurities so that we want to hold onto what we've got. A mother wants to hold onto her son, a man to his business subordinate, a teacher to his pupil. A Christian discipler wants to maintain a grip upon the young believer, and a wife wants to possess all the time her husband has to give. But all come to realize that the more they are willing to release others to the impulses of the Holy Spirit, the more they, the "releasers," are likely to receive. That is one of the strange paradoxes of Christlike love. Of course the principle works when all of the other elements of healthy relationship are in place also.

A classic story demonstrating this release comes in the life of Eli, the high priest of the temple in Shiloh, and Samuel, the young man whom he raised on behalf of his mother, Hannah (1 Samuel 3). One night when the boy rushed to his bedside thinking Eli had called him, the old man had to face the fact that Samuel was hearing God's voice. Although some might have been tempted to jealously conceal the fact, Eli told Samuel what he suspected the voice in the dark was all about. It was God speaking, Eli told Samuel, and if the voice was heard again, Samuel should answer in a particular way.

You can't help but wonder if Eli felt a bit of pain that Samuel was receiving God's special attention instead of him. Why the younger rather than the older? But Eli released Samuel to become exactly what he had trained him to be: a man in touch with God's heart. That was Eli's return on investment.

The picture of our young son and his little sister will always be a precious possession for the two of us. And each time we look at it, we see the figure of two human beings locked into a relationship—in this case brother and sister. With a grip on her wrist with one hand and a gesture of direction and determination with the other, he seems to be saying, "This is *my* sister, and I'm out to make sure that she gets where she's going." To get her there is his investment.

And that is the investment involved in all enabling relationships. When a friend, a spouse, a parent, or a mentor decides that another should be enabled to become all he was designed by God to become, watch out for the progress, watch out for the growth. It will come, and a little part of the world will become a better place.

Epilogue

For several years the telephone company has been asking us to reach out and touch someone. The fact of the matter is that Jesus Christ was calling for people to do the very same thing almost 2,000 years ago. As we've seen, Jesus made it clear that the ability to create and complete such a loop was a significant evidence of discipleship.

As we tried to point out in the earliest pages of this book, it is instinctive for people to want to reach. But touching is another matter. Almost everybody reaches, but few—relatively speaking—touch. And that fact is remarkable—and tragic. In a world where communications have been developed and enhanced, it is a massive irony that people do not find it easy to communicate.

Moss Hart told us of his deepest longing to touch his father physically and to say things that would cross the gap of hurt and disappointment between them. But he could not—perhaps because he was too young and immature; perhaps because he was afraid of being rebuffed; perhaps because his father had never created a dynamic of relationship in which a son would have felt free to do so; perhaps because Moss Hart just didn't know how to break the ice and get the job of communicating done.

We have tried to say that the gap can be crossed, that people who reach can touch and be touched. This has been our experience. And we have found that it comes with strength when ordinary people

117

choose to make Jesus Christ central to their lives and relationships. This is what happened to twelve men who accepted His invitation to follow Him. There was every reason for their loyalty to one another to have shattered, especially after Jesus left them. But the tremendous and encouraging fact is that their relationships did not fall apart but only grew stronger. Why? Because Christ was at the center of their choices, their values, their commitments.

The insights we have shared have come out of experiences with one another and with others. But our experience is not enough; what has made the astounding difference and provided the power to reach and touch in our marriage, our family, and our friendships is the power of Jesus Christ.

"We were not on that basis. . . ." Moss Hart wrote of a sad moment with his father. Christ puts people on that basis. In Him, reachers become touchers. *If those who reach could touch:* they can! We know!